HOMEWARD

Homeward

Personal Stories on the Search for Belonging

Edited by Emma Fulenwider

the Birren Center

ISBN 978-1-7379296-2-8

Library of Congress Control Number: 2022919379

The Birren Center

Laguna Woods, CA

www.guidedautobiography.com

Dedicated to Robin Lynn Brooks
1952-2022

Best Wishes
to
Connie & John

Roslyn O'Connell

Contents

Introduction

Most people are not going to write an entire memoir. Over half of the population feels that they have a book inside of them[1], but less than one percent ever reach inside and get that book out.

Luckily, memoir writing doesn't have to be all-or-nothing. Many people find satisfaction in the personal practice of sitting down to reflect and record their life experiences. Book writing is a marathon, but some of us just want to take a stroll around the block once in a while.

The Birren Center for Autobiographical Studies is an organization born out of the exciting discoveries that Dr. James Birren made in his research at the crossroads of reminiscence, story sharing, and wellness. One of the founders of the USC School of Gerontology, Dr. Birren was intrigued by the function of life stories. Why do our memories pester us? Why do humans feel compelled to share their stories?

Over the course of many years, and with the help of his research team, the general answer he found was "because it's good for us." Because processing hard things in a healthy way brings healing. Because

---

1. According to a 2021 survey conducted by OnePoll on behalf of Thriftbooks, 55 percent of those surveyed believe the story of their life should be made into a book. Out of 1,000 people who started their memoir, only 6 completed it.

releasing our story to the collective and knowing we have been heard gives us a sense of connection, validation, and relief.

Because when we listen to someone's story, the differences between us shrink and the similarities grow, giving us a sense of belonging to each other.

The curriculum that Dr. Birren developed, which we know today as Guided Autobiography (or "GAB") treats memoir writing as a means, not an end. A balm for the wounds that time does not heal, and a tool for digging up the pearls of wisdom that deserve to be saved and passed down.

I'm excited to share with you the power of these personal stories, written by people who don't call themselves "writers." Every essay in this book was written by a member of the GAB community in an effort to make sense of this life and share what they've learned with you, dear reader. Our sincere hope is that our stories inspire you to write your own.

Onward!

Emma

Part | ONE

Finding Belonging In Our Roots

Where I'm REALLY From

by Claire Tembreull

I was scanning the pool from my lifeguard chair one day when a swimmer approached the lifeguard stand. They smiled and made small talk while putting on their cap and goggles. We chatted about the weather and they asked what I was studying in school. I told them I was studying to be a speech-language pathologist. They asked where I'm from, and I told them Gladstone, a small town in the Upper Peninsula of Michigan.

They folded their arms and stared at me with inquisitive eyes, clearly unsatisfied with my answer. I felt my face flush, sensing the all too familiar question about to leave their lips: "Where are you *really* from?" I wasn't surprised by this turn in the conversation. It's a question I'm often asked while lifeguarding. However, I'm always hesitant to respond.

As I processed their question, I darted back and forth between two potential answers. I could go with the short and sweet answer, "As I said, I'm from Gladstone," or I could go a step further and say, "I was actually born in China and adopted when I was eleven months old." Do I dare give this stranger the satisfaction of affirming that I'm not really "from" here, or do I not bring it up? I fidgeted with my whistle and took a deep breath before deciding how to respond. I shared with the swimmer how I was adopted from China. Their eyes softened. "Oh, that's interesting," they said as they smiled and walked towards the pool, clearly ending the conversation.

When people make assumptions or question my birthplace just based on my appearance, I feel vulnerable and insecure about who I am. I've had conversations with other Chinese adoptees about this question that follows us wherever we go. We've agreed that it's a hard question to answer because it feels like we're giving people the satisfaction of being right. I understand people might be curious, but I don't think they realize how their words question our very sense of belonging.

The height of the pandemic brought on a new set of challenges regarding my sense of belonging. Watching the news regarding the coronavirus, I couldn't believe the poisonous words thrown at Asian Americans. I heard awful stories of hate crimes against Asian Americans and felt uncomfortable in my own skin. I was nervous and anxious in public settings, fearful of someone questioning me or my sister (also adopted from China) or telling us to go back where we came from. I've never had words of such animosity said to me, and hope I never will. The one thing I truly learned from the pandemic is that words matter deeply.

If I get another chance to answer the question of "where I'm *really* from," I know how I will respond. I will tell them I come from a family who opened their hearts and home to a little baby girl. I will share how I grew up in a community filled with the kindest and most thoughtful people, who continue to inspire me and support me in all that I do. I will tell them I'm from a childhood full of laughter, nightly bedtime stories, music, dancing, and creativity. I will say that I come from the caretakers who found me outside the orphanage when I was only a day old. Finally, I will tell them I come from my biological mother and father who live across the world in a small province of Xinyu, China. It's a family and a place I don't remember but will always be a part of who I am. I come from all of these things, each one just as important and special to me as the next.

We all "come from" more than just a physical place. We are defined by so much more. Where we come from is just a small part of our story.

The stories we share, the experiences we have, the communities we live in, and the people we're surrounded by: these things write the chapters of our incredible story. Each new discovery about ourselves is another step closer to discovering our place of belonging in this big, beautiful world.

***

Claire Tembreull is a grad student at Central Michigan University and plans to become a speech-language pathologist. She intends to conduct a thesis exploring the use of Guided Autobiography with post-stroke participants as a way of finding and rediscovering oneself. Claire enjoys playing pickleball, swimming, and spending time with friends and family. She is from Gladstone, Michigan.

Longing to Be: My Path to Mature Masculinity

by Steve Hoover

When I was coming of age, masculinity was the box that re-strained and defined who we were—and who we were not. Like the proverbial fish that isn't aware of the water, the box just *was*. For many of us, the journey was defined, the route laid out, and the outcome predestined. In order to belong, we simply needed to learn the rules, understand the dimensions, constrain our emotions, and follow the leaders.

This is the era I was born into, before there was a word for it. Later, social forces would not only identify and question "toxic masculinity," but demand that we see it, accept it, and ultimately own it.

As with many young men, my journey into masculinity started with my father. He typified the traditionally masculine male of his genera-tion. A man was a successful breadwinner, the protector of hearth and home, physically strong, fearless, emotionally stoic, sexually success-ful and lord of his domain.

As a young man, I learned the rules and roles through examples, as well as the consequences for venturing outside the box. Men don't cry: we suffer our injuries, both physical and emotional, in silence. We are self-sufficient: we don't ask for, nor do we need, help. We solve problems, we don't talk about them. Actions, not words, are our currency. We don't need to say how we feel: our behaviors speak for us. Why say "I love you" when you show it every day?

"Feelings" were for girls; boys didn't need them—they existed outside of the box. Stuff them down, shut them off, or act them out, but don't express them.

The rules for masculinity were strictly enforced by our role models and by other boys. "Be a man, men don't cry, men don't back down" were the messages men lived and died by. The rules of masculinity were also enforced by the women in our lives, although they did so reluctantly and with a sense of our loss. They prepared their sons to live in a man's world, but at the cost of raising them to be emotionally constrained.

Though I felt that mine was the masculinity I wanted, I sensed that portions of myself were out-of-bounds, relegated to quiescence. It was relatively easy to play the role, don the mask of masculinity and banter with the boys. We all knew the correct words, the acceptable attitudes. Even if none of us truly believed what we said, the risk of not belonging was too great.

We lived fully within the confines of the socially-prescribed rites of passage that marked manhood, those mileposts of significant transitions: driver's license, high school graduation, draft card, loss of virginity, drinking, college, marriage, job and children. However, unlike my father's generation and those before him, there were cracks in the edifice. As it is said, "What you resist persists."

Through the mentorship of men in my life, I became a socially acceptable man, but not yet a man-in-full. For that, I had to re-engage aspects of myself that had been subdued, pushed outside of the box. Forces, external and internal, began moving toward a crisis. For my ego to mature, I needed to be open to a different type of mentorship.

I was not alone in experiencing the changing forces that impacted men of my generation and, eventually, my father's. I was witness to the changing dynamic within my parents' marriage that should have been a call to awakening. Roles began to shift with my mother's emerging independence and my father's tightening grip on the world he understood. The crack in their relationship blew open when she responded to his latest "my house, my rules" dictum with the retort "I no longer need you." Then, in what I have come to deeply appreciate as a message of love—and, more importantly, of understanding—she added, "But I still want you."

A simple distinction of needs versus wants placed their relationship in a new configuration—one based on mutuality, not dependency. She was my first model of the emerging feminine, the archetype who serves as a guide for men to revive parts of ourselves that have been ignored in the service of the socially-prescribed myth. The anima I had suppressed began to emerge.

My second model of the secure, independent feminine who wanted—but didn't need—entered my life when I was still living the traditional masculine ideal. As I pressed up against my wife's subtle (and sometimes not so subtle) teachings of the mature masculine, I discovered the limitations of my boy psychology. Like my father, as I listened deeply to the voices for change, I was forced to reconsider and reject masculinity as I knew it and tap into a way of being that had once existed in me, and in all men.

I see this change now in my six-year-old grandson. I am hopeful as I watch his parents encourage him to live the full emotional life that his grandfather and great-grandfather had, then lost, and then finally found again.

***

Steve Hoover, retired professor, works part-time as the Healthy Aging Coordinator for the Central Minnesota Council on Aging. Former member of the Board of Directors of the American Men's Study Association, he serves on the Board of Minnesota Men's Sheds Association. He leads Guided Autobiography as well as Healthy Aging for Men. Steve lives in St. Cloud, Minnesota.

A Taste of Judaism

by Wendy Bancroft

When I was seventeen, I learned that my biological father was not who I thought he was.

I arrived home from school one day to find my mother standing at the kitchen sink, peeling vegetables for supper.

I asked how her day went. She didn't immediately respond. Instead, looking down at the vegetables in her hands, she paused and said, "Wendy, I have something to tell you."

"Yes?"

"Al McClelland is not your father."

Some might have been taken aback by this news, but I remember simply being intensely interested. Fascinated. Then again, I'd never met the man I thought was my biological father.

I said, "Oh really? Then who is?"

To which my mother replied, and the words are burned into my memory, "Your father was a very clever Jew." Wow. A strange, exciting, and intriguing response. Strange because it smacked of anti-Semitism—not typical for a mother who had raised me to have huge respect for Judaism. Exciting because that very learning had predisposed me to like the idea of being Jewish.

Intriguing because, well, it just was. *When did all this happen? Why am I just learning about this now?*

She told me the bare facts. His name was Myer Sharzer. They had worked together on a Vancouver newspaper—he as a reporter, she as a photographer. Both were married at the time, and both had children. Mother and Myer fell in love and ran off together to Winnipeg, leaving their marriages and children. There, he soon found work with another newspaper.

Within a few months, their relationship fell apart. In time, Myer became head of the Canadian Jewish Congress—but Mother was not Jewish. Even if Myer could overlook this, his family could not.

This happened soon after the end of the Second World War, when Jews were deeply scarred by the Holocaust. After returning from a family wedding that included most of his extended family, Myer broke off his relationship with my mother. I learned years later that his relatives had referred to my mother as "that woman." She clearly did not fit.

Mother left Winnipeg and reunited with my brothers in Edmonton, where they had been living with our grandparents. Mother never saw, nor spoke, with Myer again. She was four months pregnant.

I was curious to know more, but Mother had no idea where my father might be living. She thought he might have returned to Vancouver where his sons lived with their mother. I let it go.

When I was twenty-four, I was married to a researcher for CBC Television News in Edmonton. He came home one day and said, "Guess what! I think I may have found your birth father." In his research for an upcoming interview with Phil Givens, then Mayor of Toronto, David had learned that Myer was a close friend of Givens. When he saw Givens the next day, David would find an opportunity to ask him how to contact Myer. When that opportunity came, Givens said Myer had died fourteen months before.

That was almost the end of it.

Years later, when I was also working for CBC, a friend and colleague who knew my story offered to make contact on my behalf with Shirley, the woman Myer had married after my mother left. Shirley had worked with my friend Helen as a journalist at the Toronto Star. I gulped and said, "Okay." *Am I ready for this?*

I met Shirley and liked her. I also liked my new half-sister, Jacky, and half-brother Steven. By then I'd also met my half-brother Mike, Myer's son by his first marriage. I liked Mike and my cousin David, who headed up the congregation at Temple Sholom.

My Jewish world was expanding, as was my interest in Judaism. All those books and movies my mother had introduced me to when I was young had done their work. My memory cells were pushing for recognition. After attending a Rosh Hashanah dinner at the home of a friend and finding the music emotionally meaningful, I decided to look further.

I attended a series of information sessions about Judaism and liked what I heard. I highly respect Judaism's focus on social justice. I also attended several services at Temple Sholom. I loved the rabbi, and everyone was welcoming. Converts are encouraged these days, and Jewish lineage through one's father is recognized. I don't believe in God—I wish I did—but even there, Judaism suits me. You don't have to believe in God (although it doesn't hurt). But I do have to feel like I belong.

Every Jew I met, secular or religious, shared a rich multi-century history. I loved their high holidays and associated rituals. Years before, my half-sister, Jacky, had told me I could never be Jewish because I didn't have that history. Jews I've met since have told me this is nonsense, but I couldn't shake the feeling that Jacky may have been right.

The clincher came when the assistant rabbi told me that I could no longer practice Christmas (I've since learned I could have easily ignored that proviso). Christmas is not a religious occasion in my family, but we love it and I couldn't even consider giving it up. Oh yes, and this rabbi told me it would take a year of study to become a member and I would need to learn Hebrew.

I finally gave up, saying, "I don't have time to be Jewish."

But the other day I got my 23andMe results back. I am officially fifty percent Ashkenazi Jew. I'm part of a lineage that goes back centuries. At least on paper, I know I belong.

***

Wendy Bancroft's work history spans a career as an award-winning journalist with CBC Television, a researcher with two national research organizations and jack-of-all-trades in her own video production company. For the past eight years, she's been a Guided Autobiography instructor, with two of those years spent training others to teach GAB. Wendy holds a master's degree in political science. She lives with her husband on Vancouver Island.

Grandma and the Country Revival Meeting

by Larry C. Tolbert

T hat third picture on my grandparents' wall just didn't seem to fit.

I was raised by my maternal grandparents in a simple four-room farmhouse high on a hill in southern Illinois. Much like paintings, the windows and doors framed nature's art—brash summer displays of swishing creeks and deep green hills, alternating with crystal winter scenes of snow-carpeted slopes dotted with evergreens.

Inside, on wallpapered walls, were more modest displays of man-made art. The first was a reproduction of Cupid's lovestruck glimpse of Psyche, mythic characters who obviously had some serious chemistry between them. The second was a black velvet painting of Don Quixote and Sancho Panza on their way to the next fantastic adventure.

The third was a reproduction of Jesus' loving gaze, eyes almost heartbreakingly compassionate. Although all their art felt a bit out of place and time, this piece was the most puzzling because my grandparents weren't religious. No one in my family was, although my grandma was deeply principled.

A teetotaler in a family filled with "problem drinkers," as it was called then, Grandma was my rock. She was a stoic who had her values and remained true to them even when they weren't shared by others. Grandma was hard-working, self-reliant and totally unfamiliar with the finer things in life. Curiously, even though Grandma could read and write (Grandpa couldn't), I have no memory of any books in the house other than an equally incongruous Bible that had seen better days, a book we never read.

I knew my grandma had been baptized in the Lutheran Church, even though she never spoke of it. As I grew older—maybe nine or ten—my grandma, with me in tow, began attending the small Methodist Church "down the road apiece" from our house. I learned everything I know about Christianity, Methodist-style, from Sunday school classes and illustrated weekly readers the church sent to our home.

The readers were full-color, comic-book style publications with characters engaged in fantastic adventure stories—David defeating Goliath, Jonah in the body of a whale, Jesus casting the money lenders out of the temple. Those rip-roaring biblical tales gave Superman, Batman, and Wonder Woman a serious run for their money. They certainly held my attention and engaged my imagination, which made the moral message at the end of each story all that easier to take in.

I believe my grandma was concerned that I had a good moral upbringing—and perhaps not follow in the footsteps of my more wayward uncles and cousins. She must have also been concerned for my eternal soul because she arranged for me to be baptized at the very next revival meeting held in that small Methodist church.

Revival meetings were periodic, maybe once a year. Perhaps an updated count of souls yet to be saved is what triggered the arrival of the circuit-riding revivalist preacher. You see, a revival event called for a soul-saving specialist—the regular Sunday minister just wouldn't do.

When that summer's revival meeting rolled around, congregants from miles away arrived in their Sunday best, even though it was Wednesday. Grandma wore her finest old calico dress, and I was all scrubbed up and dressed in my best pants and shirt.

We solemnly took our place on the hard wooden pews. The revivalist minister started out gently, building like approaching thunder—first quiet, then ever-louder, rolling rapidly across the windrows of congregants, till he was preaching up a full-blown storm. With the emotional and physical temperature ratcheted up to a fever pitch, the minister stripped off his jacket, loosened his tie, pulled open his collar, rolled up his sleeves, and mopped the sweat from his face, never missing a beat of what he had come to say.

The church's electric fans, mightily swirling above us, were fighting a losing battle. Ushers passed out hand fans with scripture printed on the back. Men, women and children furiously fanned themselves. With the high-powered preaching and swirling fans in the hot, mesmerizing summer air, I thought we might all ascend directly into heaven any minute now, baptized and unbaptized alike, church building and all.

We didn't. But I have to give that Methodist minister credit: his sermon was impassioned and positive. The focus of his appeal was God's love and mercy, the benefits of living a life without sin, and the promise of heaven in the afterlife if you followed Jesus' example.

As positive as the message was, I must admit I didn't really have a "come-to-Jesus" moment. But I loved my grandma and wanted to ease her mind regarding the safety of my soul. So I dutifully strode to the front of the congregation along with others to have three handfuls of consecrated water placed on my head by the minister in the name of "the Father, the Son and the Holy Ghost."

To my surprise, I felt moved by the sincerity of the ritual. To my further surprise, Grandma joined me in receiving the baptismal blessing herself. Something about her gesture touched me and deepened my love for her.

I rarely cry. But when Grandma died during my senior year of college, I made the long drive back to that country church. I held up reasonably well during the memorial service. Getting into my car after the service, I broke down. I'm not sure how long I sat there alone and crying before gathering myself, starting the car, and threading my way slowly through the country roads of my childhood toward the highway that took me back to college.

***

Larry C. Tolbert holds master's degrees from the University of Illinois and San Francisco State University. He has been an English teacher in the U.S. and Algeria, a Silicon Valley marketing communications director, and senior government education developer. His works have appeared in Birdland Journal, North of Oxford Journal, ESCOM Journal and In the Wind (Las Cruces NM radio). Born and raised in Southern Illinois, he currently resides in Northern California.

5

Ash Tree in Summer

by Roselyn O'Connell

July, 1950.

A lone tree grew near the barbed wire fence outlining the cornfield of our family farm in McLean, Nebraska. After riding Spot, my pinto pony, half a mile north and then a mile west down a dusty gravel road, the small ash tree offered the only summer shade. Mom often wrapped a thick-cut baloney sandwich in crinkled wax paper for my picnic under the lonesome tree.

Grabbing Spot's wiry mane, I swung my short, tanned legs over his side until the toes of my brown lace-up shoes touched the matted grass. Safely on the ground, I sat and ate in the pleasant shade. Spot munched on the grass. His brown and white tail flicked, a metronome ridding sweaty flanks of biting flies. Green slobber ran across the metal bridle bit out the sides of his mouth. I held the reins in my hand, giving him enough slack to bury his head deep into the tall grasses but not enough for him to get any ideas about making a run for home. A typical summer day in the 1950s.

May, 2021.

I am driving to McLean where I hope to reconnect with my tree—if it is still living. Pavement gives way to gravel roads over the final five miles to the village that was once my prairie home. A place I left when I was twelve, but it never left me.

A fat raindrop slides down the windshield, like a single tear, as I roll into McLean. Not a trace is left of our farmhouse and outbuildings. Any evidence of our lives there in the 1940s and 50s has vanished. I feel a vague longing for the past...the red barn with the sloping roof and the two-story white farmhouse where the water pipes froze in the winter, where runty, rescued piglets slipped and slid across the yellowing linoleum kitchen floor and where Mom made the world's best fried chicken from the pullets she caught early in the day.

Our farm had a sheltering grove of Mulberry trees north of the farmhouse. Mulberry trees live roughly twenty-five to fifty years. No wonder the trees have since fallen down, their trunks scattered about like columns of Roman ruins. When we were young—the trees and I—they contributed their trunks and leaves to countless hours of childhood play. Tying scavenged bailer twine between their trunks, we fashioned playhouse kitchens, mixing mud pies that were plopped between the large green leaves and served up on old tin plates from the junk pile behind the corn crib. A mud sandwich to admire but never to eat.

In McLean, Ernie Voss's general grocery store has tumbled in on itself, scattering pock-marked red bricks across splintered floor planks. I study the caved-in walls like an archeologist, unearthing past sultry summer nights when we watched western movies from splintery, low wooden benches. The exterior brick wall of Ernie's store served as the screen. The movie projector sent flickering slices of light through the soft, dark night. Fireflies flirted in flashes. Tuesday nights brought farmers from a ten-mile radius to watch the free show and trade their eggs and milk for groceries. Some kids had a nickel or dime to buy popcorn, candy or pop. Practical farm women gathered in clusters to trade recipes and tricks for getting their hens to lay more eggs. Men generally convened at Dangburg's Tavern for as many cold Hamm's beers as they could drink before the movie ended.

McLean once had a jail. Few bad guys came through, but one exciting May night in 1953 two men and a woman broke into Ernie's general store. Ernie heard them talking on a two-way radio and alerted the telephone operator, Mrs. Hilda Kruse. Through the magic of the crank telephone system and the multiparty line, she called several local farmers. Adrenalin-stoked men raced their Fords and Chevys to McLean, armed with shotguns and pistols. Ernie Voss and Cliff Galvin had already cornered the wannabe robbers inside the store when the "posse" showed up. The terrified trio came out with their hands up. More than a few pairs of overalls were peed that night, but boy was it a good story.

The McLean Methodist Church now has a rusty padlock on the front door. A stately church bell sits on a base, hunkered down on the dead grass near the front door. The church used to hold Vacation Bible School each July. Children sang "We Are Climbing Jacob's Ladder" and waited for their cherry Kool-Aid in paper cups and squares of soda crackers sandwiched with chocolate frosting. I could almost hear their voices and see my Aunt Vera shepherding my brother, cousins and I into the freshly waxed wooden pews for the Lord's Prayer.

Leaving McLean, I drive up a small hill just northwest of the old farm. I drive past the tree in the same way teenage boys once drove hotrods past groups of high school girls on Saturday nights in small town America...slowly, purposely, hopefully. I pull up parallel to the tree and let the car idle. Holding my breath, I dare to look. Branches of my ash tree sway to the rhythm of an easterly wind tiptoeing through the leaves. The wind dips to lick the tops of the ditch grasses, sweeping over them like a long, wide tongue. The wind, the branches, the tall grass in the ditch all feel familiar, pulling me back through the years. I am a young girl again, leaning against my pony under the leafy tree, right where I belong.

***

Roselyn O'Connell began writing as a child. She earned an MLS from Arizona State University and is a certified Guided Autobiography instructor. She has led education and empowerment classes for women in Pakistan, Iraq, Jordan, the West Bank, Swaziland, Lesotho,

Namibia, Ghana, Brazil, Trinidad-Tobago and the U.S. She lives in Scottsdale, Arizona with her husband George and loves spending time with her children and grandchildren.

6

Maryvale

by Cam French

No matter where we journey, we are never prepared for what lies ahead.

I first saw Maryvale in August of 1958, when Nana drove us through the high, black wrought-iron gates. A larger-than-life stone guardian angel, protector of children, stood sentry. Formerly known as the Los Angeles Orphanage, Maryvale was twenty-six miles southeast of our former life in the Chino Valley.

Caroline and I, ages twelve and fourteen, respectively, passed manicured lawns and brick buildings. Fearful imaginings of a gothic orphanage quickly faded like a shadowy nightmare. Instead, it resembled an exclusive boarding school from a Hollywood movie.

Seated in a small room off the reception area, apprehension gripped us. A nervous stomach and uncertainty held me hostage. A tall, slender nun entered, a large smile across her ruddy Irish face. Reaching toward me, her hands were pale with neatly clipped nails, white moons against shell pink beds. Her arms enfolded me against her thick, blue serge habit and heavily starched linen wimple. My bones melted into the security of her embrace. At that moment, the compassion of Sister Frances McCarthy, Daughter of Charity, led me away from the misery that had enveloped me since Mama's death five weeks before. To an adolescent starved for stability, she radiated calm and safety.

Sister Frances gathered the three of us up and moved us from the administrative offices toward the dorms—our new "home." I stared at her flapping "angel wings," a white cornette headpiece. Stepping briskly on black, sturdy high-topped shoes, her long gown swooshed down the walk. She guided us across the grounds to St. Michael's Group. Wide-eyed, our legs pumped to keep up with her gait. Her stride slowed as she escorted us to our separate dorms, explaining group rules. Inquisitive, welcoming faces popped around doorways. Others offered cool appraisal.

Usually formidable as a pit bull, Nana's eyes filled with tears at our parting. She'd made the right decision, yet felt heartsore and guilty for placing us at Maryvale. However, I watched the weight of the last nine months leave her steadfast shoulders. Relief highlighted her stoic face. Her deathbed promise to our mother—never separate my girls—honored and fulfilled. That fall, hope and opportunity became our currency toward an improved future.

After settling in our dorms, I learned that the grounds encompassed a primary school, a private chapel, and an Olympic-sized swimming pool. Maryvale also provided the most modern and progressive social service programs Los Angeles had to offer its homeless and neglected female children.

Girls were divided by age into groups of twenty-four. Assigned to St. Michael's Group but placed in different dorms, Carolyn and I began settling into our personal spaces. Four dorms. Six girls to each dorm. Each dorm its own universe. Each cubicle held a single bed, built-in blonde wooden dresser, and a small closet for clothes and shoes.

Faced with loss and change, I initially lived in a state of sorrow. Those early months found me at the edge of a grief-stricken precipice. Instead of sliding down the steep incline of despair, I chose to survive. And soon enough, I learned that I lived with girls rescued from far more wretched situations than I.

Inside Maryvale's walls lived White, African American and Hispanic girls, including refugees fleeing Castro's Cuba. Some girls had lived a lifetime of abuse or neglect, wearing damage like a bruised tattoo over their shattered hearts. Others were so outwardly sophisticated and worldly, you wondered at whose knee they had learned such skillful manipulation. Their stories stung my ears, but I could not stop listening to them. Their suffering felt like my own. Young women appearing tough, yet achingly tender and just as emotionally unsettled as me. I was not alone in my anguish. For the first time in my young life, I discovered "sisterhood" with females other than my own sister. I had found my tribe.

In time, my internal clock became set to the chapel's chimes, their tolling bells differentiating between morning lauds and evening vespers, the official set of daily prayers prescribed by the Catholic Church.

I discovered that unlike our disorderly Chino household, the trains ran on time at Maryvale. With so many charges in their care, discipline was essential. Weekdays we woke at 6 a.m. with Sister lightly clapping her hands, bidding us good morning. We washed, dressed, and readied ourselves for breakfast and school. At 7:30 a.m. we left for our respective schools. Upon our return, we toiled at homework before the 5:30 p.m. dinner hour. After dinner, we washed the dishes in a steamy institutional kitchen. If homework was finished, we enjoyed free time. Lights out by 9 p.m. Early to bed, early to rise.

Besides caring for our own cubicle, Saturday chores were assigned: mopping and waxing the halls, washing windows, and cleaning bathroom stalls. I learned to wrangle the large industrial floor polisher, dipping it one way and then the other as it dragged me down the long linoleum halls, making perfectly round sweeps and swirls. As I grew older, I worked as a swim instructor during the summer. I trained on the office switchboard, a skill which could serve me outside of Maryvale.

In my five years at Maryvale, I found compassion, stability, and lifelong friendships. Within those walls I grew from adolescence to womanhood. After high school graduation, I left the safety the Sisters provided, walking through those high wrought-iron gates into a world I knew very little about, and not entirely ready to begin the next chapter. Maryvale was a safe haven, and over the many years since I left it still appears in my dreams, always welcoming me home.

***

Cam French began her creative life in early childhood and creates in artistic mediums every day. As a painter, she has participated in group shows and one-woman exhibits. She is also writing a memoir. Cam and her husband live in an old brick farmhouse, where they enjoy working together in their large garden.

The Flower Aunties

by Louise Barker

Our family was an island floating in a sea of loneliness. No grandparents, aunts, uncles or cousins sailed in our waters, but the Flower Aunties bloomed strongly in my imagination. My grandmother, Violet, had died when Mum was born and, according to my mother, she came from a large family of girls all named after flowers. The details were scant, however, and Mum was always elusive when I asked for concrete facts. "How many sisters are there? What are their names, Mum?" I'd plead. No satisfying answers came and eventually I stopped asking questions. In my childish mind they remained ethereal, pale outlines of floating flower heads with ghostly bodies draped in diaphanous fabric.

By the time I was a teenager, the Flower Aunties had gained more substance. Poppy, Daisy, Lily, Jasmine, Alyssa and Rose—six cottage garden blooms. I could see them in my mind's eye—prim, dark haired women, immaculately dressed in pastel silk tea dresses with matching purses, together on a day out in town. Their heads bobbing in unison, delighting over the purchase of a lipstick, huddling together to whisper about a handsome gentleman, giggling in delight over a shared joke.

Meanwhile, I found ways to fill the gap left by my absent elders. I adopted childless friends of my parents, who kindly reciprocated my attentions and included me in their weekends and outings. Some of my friends had extended families and, from an early age, I tried to infiltrate their family space. I relished the time spent in the company of someone else's grandparents, aunts and uncles. None of these relationships were solid enough to continue and fill the gap left in my own family, but, if only briefly, I could pretend I belonged.

I was oblivious to what drove this impulse to be included in other families, a theme I now see continued through my life as I often chose friends for their strong family networks.

The years passed and the Flower Aunties faded in and out of my mind in the bedlam of adult life. I seemed to barrel from drama to disaster, my feet in a perpetual chaotic dance. I was on fast forward but I didn't belong anywhere. One day I came across a quote, "How can you know where you are going, if you don't know where you've come from?" It resonated deeply for me and came as an epiphany ... I needed to find the Flower Aunties!

After a slow and laborious search, I eventually located the details of all of my Grandmother's siblings. There were three sisters and six brothers and not a flower to be picked among them; Leslie, Edna, Robert, Lyle, Clarence, Oliver, Harold, Mary and Lillian. I felt both saddened and strangely relieved. These were flesh and bone. These were real people and they belonged to me. More importantly, I felt I belonged to them.

Photos and anecdotes emerged to show that my mother had indeed known at least her aunties, Edna and Mary. They were well and truly alive through my childhood and other siblings of my grandmother's were alive right into my early twenties. Clarence, Harold and Lillian all lived only a twenty-minute drive from our Sydney suburb. How would it have been to spend time with them and their families, and what would have been the gems of insights and information they might have passed onto me? I worked out from genealogical clues that all of their lives had not been easy and they were a resilient bunch, especially the women. Edna was a single parent and, it being the depression, she needed to marry in order to survive. As a result, she had to put her two sons in an orphanage. Mary was childless and, when her sister Violet died in childbirth, she looked after my mother for three years, sadly relinquishing her to my grandfather who had remarried. Lillian lived with an abusive husband in a tent by the rail yard where he worked, raising her six children in a situation of great difficulty. I wondered how it might have helped me in times of struggle and challenge to know these tough and gritty people were behind me, a few still walking the earth. I don't understand why Mum denied their existence, but regardless, I'm grateful for connecting with them posthumously.

Since that initial search, my ancestors have multiplied going back for generations. Genealogical research has enabled me to know the four sets of great grandparents intimately. I particularly resonate with my great grandmothers; their struggles, frailties and their strength and resilience. The Flower Aunties, though a myth, were the seed of this journey. A journey of searching for my roots. A journey of connection and being a part of a big extended family. Through finding those that came before me, I have the surefootedness to move forward, steadily and slowly, knowing I belong.

***

Louise Barker is a practicing social worker, mother of four adult children and four grandbabies. She lives and works in the Southern area of Adelaide, in South Australia, on the traditional lands of the Kaurna and Peramangk people. Writing her life stories and researching her family history has led her on a path of curiosity and exploration about what it is to be human and experience the untold gifts therein.

8

Greenpoint My Hometown

by Linda (Wojnicki) Balfour

Once you've lived Brooklyn, its blood runs through your veins. You may distance yourself from its borders, but you recognize its edge in others. Not the metro inhabitants who play cool today, but the real everyday people who know the game because they created and lived the beat. Borders differentiated by smells of cabbage and onions fried in salt pork, with Sunday roasted chicken or meatballs simmering in garlic-infused tomato sauce. Tired grandmas looking out open windows, resting their aching arms on pillows after scrubbing hallways and stoops, yelling at children in broken English.

This is my Brooklyn. Without a watch or cell phone to keep life in order, knowing that dinner is on the table and it's time to go home. Busy streets filled with people moving in every direction, sometimes stopping for a friendly chat. Boys playing stickball while the girls scratch courts in chalk for hopscotch. Life is simple. People don't compete with the Jones' cause we don't know they exist. We're poor but at the end of day, exhausted from play, we blissfully sleep. Come morning the dance begins again.

Greenpoint, affectionately known as "Little Poland," a community of immigrants and working people, is where both my mother's and father's families settled. First and second kuzyns, ciocias, wujeks, babcia, all live within walking distance from each other. It's common to drop by to share a cup of kawa with a slice of bobka as knitting needles absentmindedly create hats and gloves for cold winter months. Three generations of love and support.

The streets of Greenpoint are laid out east-west and alphabetically named. A for Ash, B for Box, C for Clay and so on, the Mason-Dixon line at Greenpoint Avenue separating lower from upper Greenpoint. We live on Clay Street. It's an industrial area with factories sharing our space. With freshly asphalted streets, it's a great place to roller skate, commandeer a scooter or shoot cardboard ammunition from our homemade slingshots.

Historians say that Greenpoint got its name because of its lush topography. That was in the 1700s. Now it stinks, the air polluted with hundreds of factories spewing contaminated smoke into the sky. Human misery drowns itself at corner bars where downtrodden men spend hard-earned money. Teenage boys are served also, until pulled out by the ear. Too many pijaks stumble into the night carrying with them the repugnant smell of beer and urine.

We move from our four-room, coal-heated apartment on Clay Street to six box rooms on Manhattan Avenue located over Joseph's furniture store, J. Joseph's & Son Co. I absolutely hate living here. It is loud, noisy and impersonal. I long for our little hide-away on Clay. I miss playing with my friends. As I gaze out the window, I see the blacktop roofs that make up Joseph's spanning the length of the block. Feral cats lament pitifully, crying out on a hot summer night. Our only neighbor sunbathes nude not caring that I gawk at her nakedness, pretending not to see me. The tarnished lining is isolation from civilization, providing tacit permission for my brother, a drummer, and his musician friends to practice undeterred for their next gig.

In time, I learn to shut out the noise. I sleep through a steady flow of rattling buses, heavy-laden trucks, honking cars, clanging fire engines and loud pedestrians.

But I wake when I hear the whistler.

His whistle is clear and crisp. I run to the window to watch the thin, tall man with perfect posture march down the avenue. He disappears too quickly. *Please slow down, I want to hear more of your song.* I'm sad and disappointed when he's out of view.

This bustling mecca houses family-owned shops where most owners know you by name. Dad buys a grocery store in the heart of Greenpoint where the entire family works. "United we stand, divided we fall" is drilled into our heads and we know how important each individual is to "the cause." Truth is, there's no choice. But some of my happiest memories are rooted in this busy deli where customers wait in line to purchase fresh cold cuts and homemade salads. Elsie and Artie, an unlikely couple, commandeer the kitchen where they whip up delicacies of every kind, paid with bottles of Rheingold sipped between peeled potatoes and seasoned roasts. I learned much about human nature over years of dealing with the myriad personalities that walked through the door. I loved them all and truly miss some of the wonderful people we called customers.

You can't go back, but beautiful sweet memories are left of lives so well-lived. The breeze on the fire escape that offered relief from the sweltering heat, walking into a wet towel drying on a makeshift clothesline in the kitchen, watermelon on sticks, the black wrought iron stove that provided much needed warmth after a bath, Minnie the cat lapping up her milk, the whirl of the sewing machine as mama stitched our clothes, the vegetable peddler calling housewives to his bounty singing out "hey potato, hey potato hoe, hoe, hoe potatoes." All gone.

Greenpoint is a hipster oasis now, apartments with a water view renting for more than 5K a month. Fashionable clubs and cafes dot the streets and little boutiques sell $200 T-shirts that fly off the racks. Gentrification.

Life was good. We all wanted more and never realized we had it all. As they say in Brooklynese ... "Fuhgeddaboudit!"

***

Linda (Wojnicki) Balfour is a retired New York City ESL teacher. She also served as a Selector for the NYC Teaching Fellows program. She has three married children and eight grandchildren. Linda lives in Yaphank, NY in a 55-plus community which she refers to as "Camp Country Point". Her weekly activities include writing, reading, playing Pickleball, canasta, painting watercolor, line dancing, and attending various committee meetings. This is definitely her time.

9

Family Voices

by Marcy Green

Our car glides slowly into the graveyard. We are here to intern the body of my Uncle Herbert, the last of the Olsen brothers. There were nine siblings in the family—six boys and three girls—of which one aunt remains.

As I get out of the car, the first person I see is Cousin David, my uncle's oldest child. The startling blue eyes above his mask are exactly like those of his father, strong and true. As the other cousins gather round and talk, I hear their distinctive Olsen voices.

I was an only child, my parents struggling with their own problems. I believe I survived and flourished because I belonged to this close-knit extended family.

My grandparents came from the rugged northern part of Norway, famous for its mountains and fjords. They settled in the Norwegian community of Hagensborg in the beautiful Bella Coola Valley of British Columbia, Canada. Theirs was a bilingual family, with all nine children speaking both Norwegian and English.

When I was a child and the whole family gathered for Christmas Eve dinners, the house echoed with laughter, shrieks from the children, quick directions from the aunties, and deep baritone notes of the uncles arguing good-naturedly—voices overlapping and powerful.

The uncles liked to debate the proper way to cook the lutefisk ("dried cod fish soaked in lye"), a tradition from the Old Country kept firmly alive. Preparation involved much tasting, turning the forks blue.

This was a dish the children shuddered at, with its distinctively harsh, acidic taste and pungent smell. We ran away when offered a bite.

Eventually, we'd be drawn to the table by the smells of sage stuffing and roasted turkey dinner. There was silence as Grandpa Olsen solemnly said grace in his heavily accented voice.

"And God bless little Marcia,"

"And God bless Llynda..."

"Ja, ja, Ole," said Grandma if he was too slow going through the list of grandchildren.

Later, beside the glittering Christmas tree, dressed in our best party clothes, we children recited little poems or sang Christmas songs. "Away in a Manger," I warbled. The oldest of my generation, I was always expected to lead with my bit.

After singing carols together, the evening always ended with the soaring, pure soprano of my Auntie Eva, singing "O, Holy Night." It stopped my breath every time. She was magnificent.

When my father died—the second oldest and one of the acknowledged leaders of their generation—I phoned each of his siblings even though I knew the word had already gone out. I phoned to hear their voices, all with the same lilting tone. It came, of course, from the distinctive rhythm of the mother tongue. Each one spoke of their love for their brother Arnold and for my mother and me. I clung to those voices.

When I was planning my father's funeral, the funeral director suggested recorded music. I told him the family would provide the singing. And sing they did, voices in perfect harmony, high and low, moving through the beloved old hymns with feeling and power. I sang too, through my tears, sad for the occasion but happy to be lifted up by my family.

Now here we were, united again, at my uncle's celebration of life.

I watched my cousins slowly carry his coffin to the grave in the ancient way, and I thought of my other aunts and uncles.

After gently placing red roses on the casket, we drove to the funeral home for the service. My cousins delivered moving eulogies and many of us went up to speak. The Olsens never left an open mic open for long!

It was my turn. I spoke of the family gatherings when my uncle was a young, vibrant man, famous for his restless energy. I mentioned the lutefisk ritual.

I looked out at the faces, lifted up, happily receiving memories and chuckling gently at my stories.

After the pastries and obligatory egg salad sandwiches, the cousins gathered together in the parking lot, swapping stories and catching up.

Cousin David bestowed on me the title of Cousin Matriarch, after carefully explaining that he wasn't trying to call me old. I just laughed. I loved it. Helping keep the family connected warms my heart.

How lucky I have been to grow up in this loud, boisterous, loving family. There is great comfort in knowing your roots, in hearing familiar ways of talking and knowing who has inherited certain traits.

Before Uncle Robert died, I used to phone him up and he would make me laugh until I cried, detailing some of the less admirable qualities of the Olsens.

"Modesty and humility were not in our repertoire," he said, citing various examples with deadly accuracy. In our family of storytellers, Uncle Robert and my father were the best.

Now I find that I have taken on that mantle with my own children and grandchildren, telling stories of the pioneer settlers in Bella Coola.

I can still hear my children listening in awe to my father.

"Were there really grizzly bears, Papa?"

"What about the dynamite blowing up the bridge by accident?"

"Tell us about the war canoes rescuing the family from the flood!"

BIG and dramatic stories. From big and dramatic people.

And now I tell those stories at funerals and family gatherings.

I never had brothers or sisters. But, oh, do I have cousins. Now that most of the tall, familiar oaks of our childhood are gone, we still have each other.

And, yes, we are loud when we get together, and we vie with each other to tell our stories.

The voices, the memories, and the family all carry on, reminding us we belong to each other.

***

Marcy Green is a retired teacher who has always loved telling stories. As an Education and Training Consultant, she taught workshops all over British Columbia, with many hair-raising adventures along the way. She lives in Shawnigan Lake on Vancouver Island with her husband and their good dog, Roxy.

10

How I Became an Outsider

by Margaret Flesher

O n a warm Friday in March 1957, a dozen seventh grade girls crowded into the café at Warren Drug in the Village Shopping Center—a new commercial development in San Angelo, Texas. In addition to a lavish array of toiletries, beauty products, and prescription and over-the-counter drugs, Warren's served up sandwiches, soups, and fountain drinks at a U-shaped counter and several booths upholstered in pale green Naugahyde. It was a short walk from Robert E. Lee Junior High, and I was always among the group that lunched at Warren's on tuna sandwiches and Cherry Cokes.

From the beginning, seventh grade had been a year best left in the archives. During the summer, not long after my twelfth birthday, I contracted a fungal infection called San Joaquin Valley Fever. The fungus in my bronchial tubes caused violent, uncontrollable coughing—particularly embarrassing when it erupted in restaurants! The condition was treatable, but I missed the first three days of junior high. I was sure my life was ruined.

I didn't know then what "ruined" truly meant. I soon learned that my mother teaching history at my school was nothing short of hell. For her part, Mom was living her own hell, challenged by a gang of young miscreants while her marriage teetered on a precipice.

The girls who lunched at Warren Drug were a constant in this maelstrom. They were my tribe, friends since we were Brownies together in second grade right through to seventh grade Girl Scouts. But it was a large tribe, and I was never in the inner circle. A couple of new faces joined the group when several elementary schools merged into the junior high population. There was Monica, a new girl whose blonde ponytail swished away the initial envy of those who now basked in her radiance; and Diane, whose pixie cut matched her sharp features and sharper tongue. Diane had gone to a school across town, but her older sister was best friends with my longtime family friend Beth. Through this connection and, perhaps, a shared sense of seventh grade marginality, Diane became my best friend.

On this particular Friday in March, not long after the annual Fat Stock Show and Rodeo, the lunchtime conversation was of boys, teachers, and the upcoming spring dance. In the midst of the chatter, Diane called me aside to a secluded aisle, sheltered by shelves filled with toothpaste and razor blades.

"Look what I got at the rodeo!" Diane said, pulling a fat cigar from her pocket. "A boy gave it to me. I'm going to start a club and the initiation is a puff on the cigar!" Diane was glowing. Eeeeyooo. They don't call childish antics "middle school behavior" for nothing!

We returned to see the girls chattering and savoring the last drops of their Cherry Cokes. Diane's voice rose over the crowd, "Hey everyone, I'm starting a club. The initiation is a puff on my cigar! Who wants to join?"

Like lemmings, my friends—my tribe—rose and followed this pied piper right out of Warren Drug and back to Lee Jr. High. I stayed behind with one girl, the daughter of a doctor, who said, "Cigars are really bad for you." I had no such logical reason for not joining in Diane's escapade. Cigars were simply disgusting.

In every lifetime, there are moments when the world shifts. Diane, the cigar, the exodus of friends from the drugstore was my first of these moments.

Diane saw to it that I was exiled from the tribe. No one stuck up for me. No one spoke to me. A few weeks after the incident, my neighbor Cindy broke her vow of silence as her mother drove us to school.

"Diane was afraid you'd tell your mother about the cigar, and she'd tell the principal."

I had, of course, told mom. But she hadn't said a word to anyone. Either common sense told her to stay out of it, or her inability to support me in conflict situations carried the day. Maybe a bit of both. Even when Diane did not get in trouble, she remained unrelenting. I was permanently blacklisted.

I did survive, of course, with new friends. Yet an internal narrative had taken root: a lone outsider, an observer. Sometimes watching the gaiety through a window and considering breaking the glass to join the party.

Years later on a business trip, my husband Andy and I checked in at the Hôtel Richemond, a historic gem on the shore of Lake Geneva. We dropped our bags in our room and headed to the opulent dining room for a late lunch. While sipping a Kir Royale, I spotted an attractive woman sitting alone at a table for six. A bottle of Dom Perignon leaned in its silver ice bucket. The woman had finished her lunch and was enjoying the champagne in lonely, lovely splendor. She summoned a waiter who appeared with a silver candelabra, its three tapers ablaze, to light her impressive cigar—Davidoff, of course.

That, I said to myself, *is who I am, who I will be.* Alone, enjoying my decadent pleasure, creating a little drama for anyone who cares to watch.

But nothing will induce me to light up a stogie in a fancy restaurant. Cigars are disgusting.

***

Margaret Flesher is a writer who grew up with family stories and a drawer full of family photographs. She discovered the Guided Autobiography method of writing life stories after retiring from a career in corporate communications. A graduate of Vassar College and a certified Guided Autobiography instructor, she has offered GAB classes online and in person since 2018. Margaret lives in Guilford, Connecticut with her ginger cats, Murphy and Muffie.

11

Tung Tau Estate

by Angela Wong

My parents were refugees to Hong Kong from China in the 1950s. With wave upon wave of displacement, what sense of belonging could we lay claim to?

In nostalgic moments, I yearn to travel back in time to be with my friends in Tung Tau Estate. My family lived on the top floor of this resettlement estate. These estates were an early form of public housing, built for homeless refugees from China. Though you will no longer find Tung Tau Estate today, it stays alive in the residents' memories.

I lived there between 1963 and 1972, from the time I was two years old. Bonds among friends are strong when growing up in such a place. It was eight stories high with no lift. Housing units were small cubicles, each hardly more than eighty square feet. Facilities like bathrooms and laundry areas were rudimentary and communal. The kitchen was outside your unit along the corridor. Children played in the common areas together. As such, we knew everything about one another's families, their problems and challenges.

My group of friends consisted of three girls and one boy, all the same age. The boy called Shen lived next door. He was an only son, sandwiched between an elder and younger sister. We shared the same drain in the middle of our units. I remember his dad clearly before he passed away one night. He was very skinny, laid in bed all the time, and always vomited out the food he ate. Shen's mum single-handedly brought up their three kids. Our mothers were close friends, sharing the similar burden of family and children. They were very hardworking people. My father earned a meager salary as a daily rated worker. While looking after young children, the two ladies earned some petty cash from take-home piece rate work, sewing beads and handbags and assembling plastic flowers.

Among my friends, sharing came naturally. We shared everything—food, toys, and games. We shared a rented bicycle when we wanted to learn cycling because we only had enough money for one. In the learning process, I fell and hurt my knee. The scar is still visible. We fought with children in the park, we swam in the water fountain. We went up to the nearby hillside to catch small fish in the streams. We climbed through the drainage into the construction site of Morse Park. We played on the new seesaw, long slides, and merry-go-round before the park opened to the public. Childhood was colourful despite our poverty.

Looking back at those days, I treasure the relationships made. Shen taught me how to fly kites. Mixing glass with glue and paste on the kite wires, the boys tried to cut the lines of others. Kite fighting was a breathtaking scene on the top floors of housing estates.

Zoe lived a few units away from mine. I liked playing with her because she knew a lot of things. However, our younger brothers always fought with each other. Her younger brother was a crybaby, whereas mine was a strong fighter who did not cry even when hit. As a result, our mothers always quarreled and were not on good terms. Thus, Zoe and I became friends in secret. We went to the same primary school and chatted happily when we were together.

Chun was on the same floor as me but in the opposite alley. She had a younger sister with Down syndrome. I played with her sister, and she liked me a lot. Chun had a generous mother who often gave us food. We were always ravenous and grateful for whatever snacks were offered to us.

Chun, her sister, and I played dress-up. I painted old newspapers with different colours and made them into skirts. We loved jumping down the staircase, jumping over rubber band string, and hosting handstand tournaments in the common area. Our narrow corridors were beautified with plants grown in small pots. For pets, we kept small fish in glass jars and even kept small tortoises and guinea pigs. Once, I lost my guinea pig in the park. Everyone helped me look and we finally found him among the bushes.

Like the adults, we young kids knew how to share and care. To coexist peaceably in such communal living required adaptability, resilience, and friendliness. I look back fondly on my childhood. I belonged to a tribe of people who built community and made the best of their situation.

When I was eleven years old, my family was allocated to a bigger unit in another housing estate. Resettlement estates were to be demolished, and the residents were relocated. I was the first among my group of friends to move out. In the 1960s, we had no hand phone nor email. We did not have group photos either. For all our shared experiences, the only records that survive are the precious memories in our minds. We cried and promised that we would remember one another.

Dear friends, our paths have diverged. I still hold tight to this sense of common belonging no matter how Hong Kong has changed. I have a strong sense of self-worth because my friends cared for and affirmed me. I have grown to be an adult who loves life and embraces challenges with confidence. My friends, I believe that you too are thriving. I remember you and our childhood at Tung Tau Estate.

***

Angela Wong is a Laughter Yoga leader who shares the benefits of laughter to seniors and members of the Singapore Women's Association. With a degree in business administration from the Chinese University of Hong Kong, she immigrated to Singapore in 1990. She received the National Day Award - Public Service Administration Bronze Medal in 2012. In 2017, Angela retired from her work as

Deputy Director of Finance of the National Library Board of Singapore. She enjoys reading and watercolor painting.

12

Reunions

by Joshua Feyen

My parents moved our family from a Milwaukee suburb to rural western Wisconsin in November of my kindergarten year. Wanting to raise my two brothers and me in the country, they converted a dairy barn into a hog operation on a ridge dotted with century farms. I drove a tractor in the fields, fenced in and then herded animals through pastures, played and hunted in the woods and planted 20,000 trees on the untillable land. By ten years of age, I had set foot on every square yard of our 140 acres. I knew its geography by heart and felt safe on the land.

Beyond our fences, however, it took a while for my family to fit in. My parents were a little too religiously conservative for the growing hippie population, and too modern for the old farmers to immediately welcome them. Eventually my parents found common ground with both groups, and I found a few friends in school. I also found some enemies. During fourth grade, a neighbor kid threw a sucker punch, knocking the wind out of me along with any nascent confidence that I fit in.

When I said what happened, my father drove up the road to talk with the kid's parents. The dad, a school board member, told my father we didn't belong, and his kid could do whatever he pleased. I toughened myself up on the middle school wrestling squad, but a congenital hip problem returned requiring corrective surgery, after which the doctor advised me to avoid athletics.

In high school, I joined the yearbook staff, sang in musicals and ex-celled in forensics. The hallway punches continued, but being called "faggot" hurt worse. Nothing says "you don't belong" more publicly. The annoying thing was that I hadn't done anything to merit the slur, until one Friday night during my sophomore year I did fool around with my best friend. By Monday I was so terrified of what we had done—and its damaging repercussions—that I rejected and lost my best friend.

By senior year the bullying had largely subsided, and I graduated with seven good friends. For my last spring concert, I sang "New York, New York," but under my breath I hummed "Fuck you and you" to most of the audience. I chose a college three hours away, partly because I was the only person in my class who had applied there. When I moved to college, I mentally abandoned my roots. When I went home, I revisited the geography I knew, but rarely ventured beyond the fence lines.

After graduation, a flurry of high school sweetheart weddings be-came informal class gatherings. One summer, two classmates got married on the same day and both couples invited our entire class to their receptions. I crossed the state because I knew some of my gang would be there.

While I hesitated when an invitation to my five-year class reunion arrived in the mail, my success and new friends in the city had buried those early feelings of not belonging. As I approached the reunion picnic, my confidence stalled when I saw the bully. I scanned the crowd for a friendly face while old feelings got caught in my throat. When I spotted my friends, I realized that I was not there for the bully. I was there to reconnect with them.

A month after the reunion, I moved abroad for a year to work, travel, and come out as the gay man I am. A few years later, many of us gathered to bury our first classmate. At our ten-year reunion people talked about the funeral, more weddings, new kids, and I came out to my friends. A boyfriend accompanied me to the fifteenth, and the man I would later marry joined me for the twentieth.

By our thirtieth reunion I noticed that far fewer spouses attended. I think we no longer needed to impress one another with our other halves, but wanted to connect with one another instead. I enjoyed myself more so than any previous reunion. I was comfortable in my own skin and had done a lot of personal growth to let go of the bullying. Days later, a second classmate died.

A few of us attended a third classmate's funeral, and following the memorial, some of us decided it was silly to wait five years between reunions—we didn't want another death to be our next gathering. That summer, a dozen people met at a restaurant. Later that autumn, nearly twenty of us gathered for another dinner.

We celebrated vacations, grandkids and little successes. We shared health challenges, parents' and childrens' struggles, divorces and new partners. And we sent selfies and group photos to classmates who couldn't make it, reminding them that we hoped they'd join us next time. After dinner, most of us continued up the hill to a quiet bar.

As I drove through town, I thought about the personal geography I knew about my classmates. I had known most of this group for forty-five years. We knew one another's last names, siblings and parents, and who was a farm kid, who was a townie.

Taking a shortcut only locals would know, the same geographic familiarity extended to my physical surroundings. I knew the route by heart—from the shortcut and sharp corners to where buildings long gone once stood. Memories of familiar people and places combined to reveal what otherness, bullies and being gay had long obscured: this was my home.

***

Joshua Feyen has been a personal and professional writer all his life. On turning fifty, he challenged himself to write fifty memoir essays in a year to share his life experiences and lessons learned with his nephew and nieces for their impending high school graduations. He has a journalism degree from UW-Milwaukee, and now lives in Madison, Wisconsin with his husband, cats, chickens and gardens.

13

My Elusive Eden

by Dawn Robbins

A week after President Kennedy was shot, Mom scrambled to orchestrate a normal Thanksgiving. Nana stooped over a double boiler, sampling spoonfuls of gravy until it was thick and dark with just enough garlic. Dad nibbled on golden sheets of skin as he carved the turkey and we filled our plates with food. My brothers, cousins and I dined at the kids' table. Even when I craned my neck, I couldn't see Grandpops in the next room. But I knew he sat at the head of the grown-up table, as usual.

Sometime between turkey and pumpkin pie, the grown-up table fell silent. Dad rushed into the kitchen and grabbed the phone, while Mom told us, "Kids, go downstairs."

I didn't. I snuck into my brother's room and peeked through the curtains. A team of medics carried a stretcher into an ambulance. It was Grandpops. He had gotten all sweaty, then fainted, Mom later told me.

"Please don't let him die," I prayed, kneeling at the side of my brother's bed.

Grandpops came home from the hospital in time for Chanukah, but he was never the same. The stroke paralyzed his left side. He cried a lot, mostly when something touched his heart. He could no longer take us to the zoo or play ball with us and he talked a little funny.

That pretty much ended traditional prayer for me.

As a kid in Temple, I liked listening to the mesmerizing melody of prayer while decoding the squiggly letters I traced with my finger in the prayer book. But I was uncomfortable with the snazzy, suburban congregation. I didn't like dressing up and going across town on Saturdays, when friends in my neighborhood watched cartoons and played outside. And I wasn't so sure about God.

The fact is, I hated being Jewish. I hated it when kids at school told me I was going to hell because I didn't believe in Jesus. I hated my school's annual Christmas show: I never got a part and mouthed the word "Jesus" in the Christmas carols so I wouldn't have to say it out loud. I hated the way teachers singled me out every year to give a speech on Chanukah, which was only significant because of its proximity to Christmas. I especially hated the Christmas tree in our house because I couldn't explain why Mom erected one each year. On questions of religion, I'd say, "My parents are Jewish."

Years later, my friend Sharon, a child of Holocaust survivors, said to me, "Dawn, you're anti-Semitic." Her words prodded me to delve into the history of my ancestors, check out synagogues, and hum melodies deep in my soul. Once in a while, I connected with a sermon. I dated—and later married—Steve, who happened to be a Jew. But despite my best efforts, I never quite fit.

One summer weekend when Steve's daughter was ten, she came home from her mom's house crying, "Daddy, are you and Dawn really going to hell when you die?'

That's how we learned that Rachel's mom sent her to a free vacation Bible camp.

"We have no idea," Steve told her.

"No one really knows where we'll go when we die," I added. "And if there's a hell, who says who's in and who's not?"

When Rachel was out of earshot, Steve called his ex-wife to express his outrage and demand an explanation. And Steve's painfully shy mother fired off a rant, recalling how neighborhood kids used to call her a "dirty Jew" at Rachel's age.

Rachel's mom apologized and said she had told Rachel, "If there is a hell, Steve and Dawn won't go there because they're good." This and a feeble apology didn't feel like enough. "I guess I don't understand," she said.

When Rachel turned twelve, she started asking Steve and me about God, religion, and the universe. Reluctant to join a congregation, our family signed up for a no-cost, low-stakes program on creating a Jewish home.

On Friday night Shabbat, we lit candles, drank wine, and ate freshly baked challah at dinner. I loved how the candlelight reflected in our children's eyes, while we took turns lighting a candle and sharing a highlight, concern or gratitude for the week.

We marked our years with meaningful and fun holiday celebrations with friends and family. In early fall for the Jewish New Year, we swished through autumn leaves to throw stones into the river and release our burdens, dipped apples in honey for a sweet year, and vowed to be good. In spring, we feasted on matzoh, charosis, and other traditional foods for Passover, recalling when the Jews escaped from slavery and committing to fight oppression. At Chanukah, we replaced the hilarity of white-elephant gifts with stories of people who gave us light and hope during the darkest season.

I finally realized my religion: Jewish Home, passed on to me by Nana and Grandpops, Mom and Dad, and their family and friends. I didn't need a synagogue.

Not until our youngest wanted to become a Bat Mitzvah. Mona needed to study Hebrew and work with a rabbi for at least a year. Local synagogues, dubious of "drive-by" Bat Mitzvahs, were reluctant to let parents of tweens like ours join.

"Sweet-talk them, Mom," Mona asked.

The following year on a crisp autumn day, Mona stood at the pulpit, beside our female rabbi, chanting the Torah portion about the creation of the world. Friends and family from near and far filled that sanctuary.

Then, Mona shared the derasha—the lesson: "The ancient Genesis story reminds us of our collective need to rebuild and protect this Garden of Eden, our precious planet."

"Amen," I say. I am home.

***

Dawn Robbins facilitates Guided Autobiography classes from her Portland, Oregon home. When not teaching, she can be found paddling dragon-boats in the Willamette River, puttering in the garden, or dabbling in words. She lives with her husband of more than thirty years, near longtime friends, three adult children, and two adorable grandkids.

14

Ladies Who Lunch

by Noelia Rodríguez

I have often considered myself an outsider—someone who belongs neither here nor there but has the empathy to connect with others.

Born in a Texas border town, I'm one and a half generation American. My mother's family has lived on the US side of the Rio Grande since the early 1900s, while my father's family has lived on the Mexico side. My mother graduated high school; my father completed third grade.

When I was five, my parents mustered the courage to move our family to Los Angeles to give me and my younger brother and sister a better chance at life.

A shy child on the first day of school, I knew I was different from the other kindergarteners. I didn't speak English. In the 60s, there was no such thing as ESL. I did not belong. I didn't want to. I learned to persevere. I learned the cash language.

Decades later, I entered a career in politics, a world where I was the ultimate outsider. I was recruited as press secretary for the Mayor of Los Angeles—a Republican, which I only mention because I was a Democrat. In January 2001, my political career ascended the ultimate rung on the ladder: the White House. Though I was still a Democrat, my Texas roots gave me an instant connection to President and Mrs. Bush.

It was after my White House tenure that I had an experience that gave me a strong, personal bond with Texans outside my family.

In 2007, I went to Dallas at the invitation of a women's charity organization to serve as keynote speaker for their annual fundraiser.

Before I arrived, I remember thinking that, had my parents not moved their young family to Los Angeles decades earlier, I would have never realized the professional success that now merited a speaking invitation from this influential civic club.

Apparently, I was a huge draw; there were hundreds of guests in the audience—mostly women. They were dressed in the finest St. John knits, Gucci bags, Manolo Blahniks and Christian Dior makeup. The perfumes wafting throughout the room were enough to make my head spin. To this day, when I catch a whiff of Thierry Mugler's Angel, I am immediately taken back to that Dallas country club.

And I smile. I smile because I think about how these women's lives were so different from my own. Yes, I had my own brands: Nordstrom suit, Donald Pliner shoes and Bulgari eau de toilette (not perfume). But I was definitely not cut from the same cloth.

I may have been invited, but I was not sure I belonged.

Most of the ladies in the audience had Mrs. before their names, while "Ms." came before mine. They were ladies who lunched. I was the main course.

They wanted to hear about my White House experience as Press Secretary to First Lady Laura Bush. As a "Bushie," I had instant gravitas. I was their one degree of separation from the President and the most powerful person in his world, Mrs. Bush.

I could have regaled them with stories of state visits, world travels, East Wing initiatives, and, of course, that life-altering day of 9/11. But I wanted to connect with these Texans. I wanted a connection of the heart.

The day before my speech, I visited over Starbucks coffee with my longtime friend Valerie, a former California colleague and Texas transplant. As I sipped my latte, I noticed my coffee cup had a quote printed on it. It was part of Starbucks' "The Way I See It" campaign, with quotes from pop culture icons. On my cup was The Way I See It #205:

> Many people search blindly for the "meaning of life." What they don't seem to understand is that life does not have meaning through mere existence or acquisition or fun. The meaning of life is inherent in the connections we make to others through honor and obligation.

The quote was by Dr. Laura Schlessinger.

Although I suspected that not many of my soon-to-be friends were Dr. Laura followers, I knew I would weave this quote into my remarks the next day. I wanted to talk to these women in a way that connected with them as individuals. Not as the first wives, arm candy or uber volunteers that I assumed they were (as I write this, I am embarrassed by my judgmental bias.) But mostly, I wanted to honor them for their charity work and their power to be forces for good.

The next morning—April 16, 2007—a Virginia Tech student went on a campus-shooting spree, killing thirty-two people and wounding seventeen others before taking his life. It was the deadliest US mass shooting to date.

The news was sobering.

After I was introduced, I asked for a moment of silence on behalf of the victims and families at Virginia Tech. The quiet was deafening. I sensed unity, a sisterhood with the women before me.

Like the tragic events of 9/11, I sensed this emotional moment would lead to the heartfelt connections I was looking for. I shared the story of 9/11 and how we, as a nation, come together in times of crisis and moments of despair. And how proud I was to be back home in Texas, where I got my life spirit.

Then, I pivoted to Dr. Laura's quote.

In the end, the ladies thanked me with thunderous applause. My heart was full. I knew that the meaning of life truly is inherent in the connections we make to others through honor and obligation.

At that moment, these were not merely ladies who lunch. They were women with purpose. Fate brought us together that day; and for a brief time, we belonged. Together.

***

Noelia Rodríguez is chief of staff for Metrolink and a Fellow at University of Southern California's Center for the Political Future. She has worked in politics and public service since the '90s, including LA City Hall, the White House and Harvard. A native Texan, Noelia is still searching for the perfect pair of cowboy boots. Preferably with the perfect cowboy in them.

15

The Dust Settles

by Brianne "Rickie" Ellsworth

I dream to be not bound by this body.
Moon-mad, vagabondage in my veins.
Miners in my lineage, my earthly blood,
I inherited Grandpa's enchantment.
His dogged smile discovering fool's gold.
Dirt diggers who then became launders,
Of clothes that is.
And here I sit,
I've been in one place so long
I forgot vagabondage is in my veins.

Out on the ocean, we are greeted by a pod of hundreds of dolphins playing in the waves. We all point and grin, awed and comforted by this fortuitous omen. The boat slows to a stop. Voices hush and my mother reads a poem. I look into the plastic utilitarian container which holds the physical remains of Grandpa Sam. As my eyes adjust to the contents, it occurs to me that I've never seen a cremated corpse before. I had imagined fine ashes like the kind cleared out of a chimney. Instead, I find coarse dust, bones and pebbles that have been waiting nineteen years to be released.

I pick up the silver metal scoop and fill it. I see black hairs and wonder how they got there, how they escaped the fiery transmutation.

I wonder if they are his or little stowaways from some other departed because I remember him with gray hair, not black. My attention drifts. *Why is it that hairs not connected to a body seem so foul?* I scold my scattered thoughts. I'm trying to be here, in my body, in the moment. I want to connect with Sam, but he feels far away.

I'm suddenly aware of my family's presence—that I'm being observed in a moment not meant for display. I take a deep breath, focus, and discreetly talk to Grandpa Sam. A prayer for just him to hear. I cast his ashes overboard, ready to watch them dance in the wind and drift off but instead they dive into the ocean, a transient float before sinking down below.

Sam was a drifter; he belonged nowhere and everywhere. Traversing the land by foot or in his motor home or truck, he wandered in search of gold. His grin conveyed certainty that there was always a treasure to be found, just around the corner. Though he panned and panned, the gold he sought was never discovered. Or was it? Maybe the seeking was the reward, for this was the life he chose.

The road became his home. He would not be confined by the house he bought with his young wife, leaving behind three children. He would not be at his daughter's wedding to walk her down the aisle. Yet Grandpa would magically appear at our door when I was a child, sometimes with fish he'd caught from the pier by our house. Always with a story, a smile, and dreams of riches. Playful and boisterous—even in his persistent alcohol haze—his words slightly slurred, especially when he took out his dentures to show us his toothless grin. His brown eyes squinted and shone as he sang and played the piano that gathered dust in our house. Once I was stirring cookie batter in the kitchen when Sam began to sway and sing, "Hey good lookin', what you got cookin'? How's about cookin' something up with me?" We all laughed and sang the chorus again together. He embodied the optimism of youth—always beaming, having fun and making people laugh. He discarded worries for possibilities and society's security for his own sense of freedom.

Death as a finality is false. There is no ending. Grandpa Sam has been gone for nineteen years, yet here we are, with him. Even as his ashes are swallowed by the sea, he lives on in my memories, in the memories of my family, and now on this page. I feel him every time I hear Hank Williams sing.

I set the scoop back into the box of Grandpa Sam and the family takes turns until the box is empty. He is, once again, free.

Unlike Sam, our family holds tight to our possessions. We are all accumulators. Houses brimming with heirlooms passed down through the generations. Collectables and antiques we hope future generations will keep, bought with money earned from stable jobs. Objects become time machines, mementos of a person, a relationship, a family history. We hold on to them, as if letting go equates to the loss of a loved one. We carry the emotional weight of that which we can't bear to forget. Dust settles.

It wasn't just Sam waiting in the clutter of my parents' garage. Stored in similar plastic containers were Grandpa Joe and Uncle Matt, respectively shelved for twenty-four and thirteen years. Today, we release their ashes too. We also remember Uncle Craig. His body was never found, assumed to be lost to the waters of Hawaii on a day of fishing from which he never returned. On this day, we let go. I let go of a grandfather and an uncle on my maternal side and a grandfather and an uncle on my paternal side, the symmetry uncanny.

I sit back on the cushioned bench of the boat and bob with the waves, thinking of Sam and Craig fishing in solitude yet never alone. Like them, I seek seclusion in nature when I need connection. I welcome the sun on my skin, the ocean sounds, the scent of salt water in the air. Embraced by nature, I am reminded that solitude is an illusion.

I observe my family and how we are woven together by our mannerisms and physical characteristics. We are tied together in familial knots, connected despite varying personalities, mismatched hobbies, and contrasting personal views. In this moment, I revel in belonging and not belonging, all at the same time. I am the granddaughter of Sam Redman, a dirt digger and gold seeker.

I've got vagabondage in my veins.

***

Brianne "Rickie" Ellsworth brings her knowledge of spirituality and creativity into the writing classes she hosts in Southern California and online. She practices writing as a tool for healing, self-care, authenticity and expression. When she isn't teaching classes, you can find her walking barefoot in nature.

16

One of the Last Male Domains

by Tony Kvedar

Nestled in the foothills of central Vermont, in the town of Bethel at the foot of Paul's Peak, was a red cabin. Built in 1957, this wooden structure was about forty feet long and fifteen feet wide. The front door opened to a large space containing a kitchen, dining room, and living room. Across the back wall to the right was a large dining room table that could seat sixteen people. Down the hallway were three bedrooms and a bathroom. Each bedroom contained two sets of bunk beds and a small bureau and could accommodate four hunters staying overnight. The cabin was built for twelve occupants; however, on the season's opening weekend, it would house at least sixteen. This was Camp Buckhorn.

Back in the 1950s, 60s, and 70s, only men were allowed during hunting season, which started the second weekend in November and ran for sixteen straight days.

I first accompanied my father on this autumn ritual when I was thirteen years old. It was a rite of passage—had I been a girl, I would not have been included. Hunting camps were for men.

The men who came to hunt were a fun-loving group. They were old friends of my dad's and had a fondness for playing poker. I often wondered which activity was of more importance, hunting or cards. Joe Stanko stood about five-foot-ten with a big round face and a stomach to match. He was a jolly fellow who loved to tease, and he was the most successful hunter and poker player of the bunch. There was Joe's next-door neighbor, Skip Sawyer, who loved to keep me on my toes, and Angelo Ribbi, who had a big nose, a cast-iron stomach, a loud voice, and a heart of gold. We spent many an enjoyable evening around the dining table with the sound of clinking poker chips, the smell of cigarette smoke, and the air blue from the cursing.

On the opening morning of hunting season, we would be awakened at 4 a.m. by someone yelling, "Where's my breakfast!" Soon, the coffee was percolating, and the smell of fried bacon filled the camp. As we ate a breakfast of bacon, eggs, and toast, another hunter shouted, "Chase the cow down here" (pass the milk) as excitement filled the air.

Out the door, we went into the cold autumn air before sunrise. I climbed up Paul's Peak while the other Buckhorn men hunted elsewhere. The sun rose in the eastern sky as I ascended the mountain. Then a rifle shot exploded into the quiet dawn morning. Streaking down the hill was a deer. It flew by me so fast that I hardly had time to raise my Winchester rifle. The animal ran down the mountain and out of sight. A few minutes later, a hunter I did not know came by and said in a thick Vermont accent, "Yep, it was a spike horn, ya know." A spike horn is a male deer with horns three inches in height. Rats, I had missed a chance to bag a deer. Somehow word made its way back to Buckhorn, and I received much teasing that night. Skip let me have it with both barrels.

The next day, Skip was hunting in a thickly wooded area. As the story was told to me, he saw several deer walk past but had trouble seeing the tops of their heads. Before he could fire his rifle, he needed to see the deer's antlers, as a hunter could only shoot a deer with horns. No matter how he twisted and turned, he could not see the tops of their heads. He told us he was certain that at least one of the deer was a male, "I could see his testicles!" He did not get off a shot, and the deer escaped.

When we returned to camp for supper that evening, Skip told us his tale of the buck that had eluded him. Chuckling, I slowly strolled to him and said, "Welcome to the club."

***

Tony Kvedar is a retired accountant and adjunct college instructor who served twenty-two years in the Vermont National Guard. A member of the Bloomingdale Writers family and "Write On" writing group, he published his first book You Sound Like a Man with a Paper Ass *in 2020. Tony lives in Florida with his loving wife Linda, they have four grown children and six grandchildren.*

17

FACES

by Beverli Barnes

1974, in the heart of downtown Vancouver, there was a black door at 795 Seymour Street. It had a poster-sized blacked-out window that opened like an advent calendar.

"Knock, knock."

The window opened and I remember being greeted by a handsome young dandy decked out in satin, glitter, a touch of rouge on his chiseled cheekbones and a soft feminine voice. In the background, the distinctive vocals of Patti Labelle spinning on the turntable, "Hey sista, go sista, soul sista, flow sista".

Of all the bars in the gay district, FACES was my favourite. It was small and intimate. Everyone knew each other. It was like family. My second family. Every time I walked into the club, I felt relieved. Like I could totally be myself.

"Gitchie, gitchie, ya-ya, da-da..."

Once inside, the dance floor was up front and centre, raised two feet so one had to step onto it like a stage. It was a smooth hardwood floor with an oversized mirror ball hanging above. Lights reflected off the ball, flickering and revolving like a galaxy of stars around the dance floor, walls, and me. Slightly larger than a billiards table, it was amazing to see how many bodies could pack onto that floor.

D.J. Susan was parked behind a counter adjacent to the dance floor, surrounded by stacks of vinyl records. Her long brown hair swayed to the beats with a perpetual smile on her face. Most nights, she would warm up the crowd with the entire Marvin Gaye anthem "What's Going On." Still one of my favourite albums of all time, the lyrics brought the clubgoers together—mostly men with a scattering of women.

The musky scent of patchouli —or "patch", as we called it back then—wafted off the hot, sweaty bodies as we grooved to the tunes. We were completely immersed in the music, base thumping from our platform boots to our hearts and souls.

Gloria Gaynor belting out "Never Can Say Goodbye," followed by Evelyn Champagne King's "Shame" and KC and the Sunshine Band's "That's the Way I Like It." Bumping and grinding, laughing and hugging, with flamboyant gay men decked out in velvet bell-bottoms, sequins, and feather boas. I was in my element.

There were barely a handful of people inside when I arrived around 9 p.m., but by 10, FACES was packed with the regulars who had befriended me from my first visit. I was only fourteen, but my fake I.D. said otherwise. I was usually a somewhat shy teenager, but in this place, I came to life!

One of the friends I made quickly was Bobby. A sweet little man, perpetually smiling and giggling like a little girl. He had deep, dark brown eyes and a mass of golden curls framing his round face. His tall, strikingly handsome boyfriend, Randy—who renamed himself "The Lux Zircon"—often wore hip-hugging wide-flared Howick jeans, an open white linen shirt, and a monstrous Navajo turquoise and silver necklace that covered his bare, leathery tanned chest. The boys would spend summer days tanning at the nude Wreck Beach before making their way to the club.

I had a secret crush on The Lux Zircon, as did most of the regulars. One look into those mischievous emerald eyes and I was mesmerized.

When Randy and Bobby sniffed cocaine, I would occasionally be invited to join them in the bathroom located directly off the dance floor. Everyone knew what was going on; but if one was fortunate enough to get an invite from The Zircon, it meant you were cool.

My first female crush at FACES was Janice, a tall indigenous woman I immediately fell for. Then there was Smokey, a dark-skinned, smooth-talking, almost bald lesbian. She invited me to visit her in the Castro should I ever make my way to San Francisco—which unknown to my parents, I did.

Barry White's deep, sexy vocals drew us to the floor like a sensual magnet. It was an intimate party of people who loved to dance.

As the crowded dance floor packed even more bodies of velvet, satin, glitter and smiles gyrating to the rhythm and blues of drums and bass, I felt an envelope of acceptance surround me. I never wanted to leave. I craved this place, these people. There was no hatred, jealousy, or judgment. These were my people. My tribe.

It's April 2022, and emotions of those days resonate when I listen to the old R&B that once flooded that tiny dance floor. I wish I could go back in time to that feeling and those beautiful people.

FACES closed in 1985 after being slated for demolition. The black door is gone. The gay bars as I remembered them are gone. Sadly, the once vibrant gay community has been replaced by steel and glass towers.

Now approaching sixty-three, I don't miss going to gay bars; but I do miss tearing it up on the dance floor, surrounded by smiling happy faces.

Nostalgia has its place. As long as I have memories of those magical nights at FACES, I am at peace with the world.

***

Beverli Barnes is a fashion designer specializing in custom courtroom attire and regalia who gained recognition for her classic white men's shirts in the 1990s. She attended the prestigious Parsons School of Design and was nominated for Entrepreneur of the Year in 1996. Beverli lives in North Vancouver, B.C. with her partner Deb, dog and cat. An avid trail and track runner, she is writing her first memoir.

18

The Library

by Lori Stokan Smith

My mom often took me to the public library. She didn't drive a car back then, and we didn't have a second car even if she did. Mom and I would walk up Butler Street past the brick row houses, the smell of stale beer from the bars, the Teamsters Temple filled with union men fighting for their rights, G.C. Murphy, Kay Drug Store, and the Community Savings Credit Union. We'd breathe in the bus exhaust, unnoticed by our hardened nostrils, accustomed to the soot and smoke. We ignored the white noise of car horns and delivery trucks backing up—*beep, beep, beep*. We walked not for exercise or our waistline, but because that's what lower to middle class people did in 1970s Lawrenceville.

It was all good, nothing to complain about. I might have even scored an ice cream cone from Vir-Lee or a Klondike Bar from Isaly's on a muggy Pittsburgh day. We turned uphill on Fisk Street, away from the Allegheny River and the steel mills toward fancier row houses with wrought iron fences and cement planters at the entrance way. These houses must have been a sight in their heyday, but now needed paint and brick pointing. There may not have been money for frivolity, but the women of Lawrenceville—with roots from Poland, Germany, Croatia, Ireland, and Italy—made sure their sidewalks were swept clean daily.

The immigrant spirit ran deep in my neighborhood. In the 1970s, some women still wore babushkas and mid-calf length dresses, and mostly spoke Polish. All of us were one step away from the old country.

We walked up the steep hill until we came upon the welcoming wooden door of the Lawrenceville branch of the Carnegie Public Library. The second American public library, Andrew Carnegie opened our branch for the mill workers in 1898.

Once inside, my mother and I parted ways. Although there was no air conditioning, the high ceilings and open space felt cool after our trek. Mom headed to the adult stacks, searching for tales of romance and mystery with hopes of finding the excitement in the pages of a book that she wasn't finding in her role as a housewife.

I took a right turn to the children's area, not looking for anything specific but finding words and artwork, rich stories and treasures. I knew every inch of my library. The children's room felt safe and happy, bright and peaceful. I felt like I belonged there. Just to be in the room was a gift. Thank you, Mr. Andrew Carnegie, who was the first to add a children's reading room to American libraries. I forgive your sins, which broke the backs of many steelworkers.

My library card was mine and mine alone—my first identification card. I felt like I was *someone*. I would grab a pile of books and then find my mother, who would be juggling a stack of ten or so thick, hardcover books of her own. In my memory, I can still see Mom waking up at 5 a.m., sitting in the kitchen, reading and drinking the blackest of coffee. Even as a child, I could tell that my emergence into the kitchen was a disappointment as suddenly her world was no longer in faraway places or romantic trysts, but rather in cleaning load after load of laundry for eleven people, deciding what to cook for dinner, and figuring out how to stretch Dad's meager paycheck.

When I became a stay-at-home mother, libraries were an integral part of our children's lives—and a respite for me. Moving to Georgia with two kids under the age of two was hard. Some days, I felt trapped in my house. I didn't know anyone, but I knew the library. Story Hour was a godsend. Anna was captivated by the librarian's words. She intently studied the pictures when the librarian turned the book in her direction. We would go home with fifteen or more books. I'd read to the kids before their afternoon nap and Jim would read to them every night before bedtime. If we fell asleep reading, we'd wake to see Anna holding the book herself and looking at the pictures.

As Connor grew, it was harder and harder to find books interesting to boys. Through the grapevine of mothers, I learned of great books my son and I could enjoy together: Gregor the Overlander, The Lightning Thief, and, of course, Captain Underpants.

As the children grew and school required more attention, reading often took a backseat until Harry Potter entered our world. True to form, the public library rose to the frenzy. Anna attended a Harry Potter event at the Bloomingdale library, complete with stations for potions, wands, and a sorting hat. The library became a magical place that evening, although most knew it was always magical. The library gives everyone a sense of belonging.

The library showed us the world beyond our neighborhood—the magical and farcical, the happy and disturbing. It helped us make sense of the world one page at a time. Our childhood was enriched each time we borrowed a special book and set foot in another world. When we couldn't afford to travel to other places, we could still explore new worlds through library books. Because of the library, we were never impoverished.

***

Lori Stokan Smith is a Birren-certified Guided Autobiography Instructor, a Life Story Writing Instructor, and a facilitator of writing groups. A published author, her work appears in How I Met My Other: Furry Friends, True Tails *and* Onward!: True Life Stories of Challenges, Choices & Change. *Lori grew up in Pittsburgh, became an Army officer, and helped fight the Cold War in West Germany. She later became a veteran, military spouse, mother, and committed volunteer. Writing is her passion.*

Part | TWO

Discovering Belonging In Our Travels

19

Everything Under Heaven

by Nicholas Hormann

I 'm touring China as an actor, having just given a performance in Guangzhou. Young people are gathered in the lobby—chatting, joking, smiling at my Chinese. A faint aroma of garlic hangs in the air. A comfortable, familiar smell. For an instant, I am transported to a classroom in Tunghai, forty-three years ago.

I had just graduated from college and was headed to Taiwan for a two-year teaching fellowship at a Chinese university. Sweat rolled down me as I poured over Chinese flashcards in a rented room at Yale. New Haven sweltered that summer. The flashcards wilted in my hands.

In October of 1966, I landed on Wake Island in the Pacific. Men in white Bermudas refueled the jet. The sky blazed. We stepped out briefly—the heat slapping us in the face—and returned to find that my flashcards had been swept out by the Pan Am cleaning crew. As we lifted into the blue, I thought of the ancient Chinese phrase tian xia—"everything under heaven"—referring to the whole known world with China in the middle. I turned the phrase over and over in my mind. Would I find my place in the Middle Kingdom? Self-regard ruled out prayer at that moment. I was too much the center of my own universe. My stomach churned. I felt lost.

In the clamor of Taipei, I somehow found a train for Taichung where I located a bus to Tunghai University—a bus that almost certainly held at least one goose and a chicken. I carried a suitcase and a portable typewriter.

Alone in the campus guest house that night, I heard cicadas in the dark, and suddenly I choked. *What am I doing here?* And I wept.

The next morning, with a fresh breeze blowing in the window, my spirits lifted a bit. Every single thing was new and strange, but I began to see possibilities. Strangers would become my friends. I might view the world through their eyes. I'd make discoveries. I drew hope from these prospects and happily brushed my teeth in tap water—water that I should have boiled first.

That morning I breakfasted on sweet bean soup and fried dough—you tyaur, a Beijing specialty.

By the next night, I had moved into the bachelor men's residence. My single room held a wooden bed, a desk, and a chair. I put a sheet on the rattan bed frame and slept pretty comfortably. It was like sleeping on tatami.

A centipede greeted me.

I took up practicing tai-chi chuan with Lin Hsun-fu, a graduate assistant in the foreign languages department. I'd shadow his movements on the tennis courts in the soft, early morning air. Lin moved smoothly through the ancient patterns. I was awkward. Big. American. Lin's mind seemed both here and elsewhere, inhabiting this world and another. This was new to me, being both present and distant. When we finished, he didn't comment. I viewed him as a Confucian gentleman, combining inner virtue with outer serenity and polish. I admired that. I very much wanted to emulate him. It seemed beyond my reach.

Lin gave me my Chinese name. First he proposed "Ten Thousand Rainbows." Rainbows have ancient symbolic meaning. But the name made the young Chinese office workers laugh. It sounded twee to them, maybe sissy.

Eventually, Lin hit on something that approximated my own name and was still poetic. I'd be known as He Yi-shao. It means "talented one." I was sure I wouldn't measure up—I'd have almost preferred being known as the slightly goofy-sounding ten thousand rainbows guy—but it hardly mattered. Most days I was "Mr. Hormann" or just "Nick." I was twenty-one, after all. My students were eighteen. They learned that they didn't have to rise from their desks each time I entered the classroom. They gathered around my desk after class, chatting casually, respectful but relaxed. They smiled at my Chinese, clustering close. The pungent aroma of raw garlic filled the air. All was well.

On name-giving day, rainbow images lingered in my mind as I gazed on rice fields, jade-green and vibrant, extending to the distant mountains. In the year ahead, rainbows often floated on the landscape: symbols of universal harmony, sometimes followed by monsoon rains. In 1544, the Portuguese named this place Ilha Formosa, "beautiful island." The island stretched before me on name-giving day, still unfamiliar and a bit mysterious. But on that particular morning, the sun flashed briefly and Taiwan sparkled. In that moment, everything under heaven seemed to hold promise. I'd find my place here. Everything under heaven included me. Tian xia.

***

Nicholas Hormann has appeared in over a hundred plays on and off Broadway and in the nation's leading professional theaters. His numerous television appearances include Modern Family, Parks & Recreation, and Seinfeld (as Calvin Klein). He attended the Yale School of Drama and was raised on fish and poi in Manoa Valley, Hawai'i.

20

Echoes

by Deborah "Devora" Ross

"**W**here's your father?"

"Why don't you have a father?"

My back is pressed up against the stucco wall of my grade school in the affluent Berkeley Hills, where my mother had been determined to rent a house for the two of us.

I want to disappear into the wall, to become the wall, solid and confident like all the other walls. My arms are crossed in front of my chest, holding and protecting me, keeping their words out.

These girls are dressed in brown skirts and short-sleeved brown blouses. Brownie uniforms. I am a Camp Fire Girl. We dress in white shirts and blue skirts. I know these girls—they are in my class, but I am not in their group and they are not my friends. I lower my head in shame as they continue to pepper me with questions.

"Don't you have a father?"

"Where is your dad?"

I don't know the answer. But their questions point out something true, something I already suspected: *there is something wrong with me.* I am different from everyone else, my family branded as deficient. One of the girls yells out in a high excited voice, "My mom said that she wouldn't let me have an overnight at your house because no man lives there. She says it's not safe!"

I feel tight inside. Tears squeeze out from my eyes and drain down my cheeks. Desperate to escape, I butt my way through the semi-circle of brown shirt tormentors, bolt from the schoolyard, and run for home.

The next day, my mother tells me that she called the Brownie group leader and complained. I digest this and wonder what will come next. My mother leaves the girls' questions unanswered. No one apologizes or makes amends. Everyone moves on, leaving the scene echoing in my ears for years to come.

World War II blew up society and the culture of Eastern European Jews. It left my mother traveling in search of safety through Japan, Shanghai, Mexico and finally America. Although she professed her love for the United States throughout her life, she never found where she fit in.

My mother's Mexican skirts, large hoop earrings, dark hair and eyes, along with a heavy Polish accent and dramatic personality, gave her an exotic flavor. The addition of divorce and a home with no father escorted me to the margins of the conventional world in 1961, fueling my own search for belonging.

With no connection to extended family or a larger community, I had little to ground me, to tether me to a history, to hold me in a container of connection and identity. I had nothing to counter the marginalizing messages.

Wikipedia defines belonging as "the human emotional need to be an accepted member of a group, part of something greater than themselves."

I longed for something beyond myself to connect with, where I could be safe, where I wouldn't feel ostracized for not having a conventional family. Over time I grew to identify with the marginalized minority and the powerless.

Craving the freedom to explore, I left home at seventeen to search for my place in the world. I did not understand at the time, but now realize I was searching for the lights of my family who had been so cruelly extinguished in the Holocaust. The air of my childhood was thick with the smoke from those snuffed out flames.

My feet carried me down windy roads where peril lurked around each blind bend. My internal GPS system had been compromised by early traumas; I was not yet able to safely navigate the terrain or identify dangerous dead ends.

Early efforts to make my mother happy bolstered a growing sensitivity and openness, which generalized to the people I encountered in my adventures. Despite exposure to the dark and painful side of life, I felt a deep, expansive compassion for humanity while exploring the edges of a world full of petty criminals, hustlers and drug dealers. With time, I learned to view myself through the same compassionate lens.

Most people I encountered had felt pushed aside and dismissed by the majority. I learned that past trauma was common and we all had the same human longings—to be an accepted member of a group, to quiet the internal voices and soothe the internal pain.

My mother's journey reverberates within my search and I see my journey as an echo of hers. The Holocaust ripped her from her world and threw her to a distant, unfamiliar shore. With no anchor, she was left to hold the murder of her mother and brother and the disappearance of her father and her entire world in a vacuum, drifting with each chilling wind of circumstance.

I am named after my grandmother, Devora. Her spirit led me to discover Judaism, join a Reform Synagogue and connect with other children of Holocaust survivors. Eventually, I came home to the world of ancient Jewish Mysticism and meditation that flourished before the Holocaust. I connected with Jewish Renewal, Neo-Hassidism, and the larger Jewish Community. I belong here, holding my mother, grandmother and all who came before me close to my heart. They led me and I carried them; together we have returned to the rich connection and identity of our ancestors.

***

Deborah Ross is a writer, artist and facilitator with a master's degree in clinical psychology. Her work has appeared in local publications and galleries. She signs her creative work as Devora, in tribute to the memory of her grandmother for whom she is named. Deborah, along with her husband and two dogs, splits her time between Vancouver and Salt Spring Island, Canada. She is currently working on her memoir.

Smokin' with the Boys in the Cattle Car

by Tony Nauroth

From the time I was a young child, I remember waking up to the discordant hacking of my mother and father as they reached for their first of many cigarettes, smoked daisy-chain fashion throughout the day.

My sister, Barbara, and I led a furious campaign against this self-destructive behavior, especially after we became teenagers and took oaths to never smoke. We tried many times to get our parents to stop, to no avail. They wouldn't—or couldn't—citing the amount of pleasure they got from smoking.

My father's coughs were the most awful, relentless even. They were attacks against his lungs and sounded as such. "HaKaaack! HaKAAAAACK!!! KaaaCKKK!!!!" and he'd light up another cigarette. He smoked two packs of L&Ms a day.

My mother's hacking was more delicate, but deeper. She smoked Pall-Mall cigarettes—*four packs a day*. Unlike my father, she inhaled deeply. "Keh! Keh!! HZAAKeeeeHeh!!!! Keh."

My parents' smoking (and my oath not to) came to the front of my brain on a cold February day in 1975. I was riding in a military vehicle with thirty-five other soldiers to the ranges of Fort Dix, New Jersey, for Basic Weapons Training.

The Army's official name for these trucks was "Army Mass Transport Containers," or AMTRACS. But to the everyday soldier who had to ride in them, they sure looked and felt like cattle cars. They were metal-sided, multi-wheeled trailers hauled by smaller-than-normal tractor cabs. They looked similar to the trailers you see on highways where, if you look closely, you can see cattle hooves, pig snouts, or horse manes between the metal slats. Only the AMTRACS didn't have slats. The sides, front and back were solid sheet metal, with four small, sliding windows rusted up. The doors opened into a metal-floored, multi-level space with floor-to-ceiling poles for soldiers to grip on to.

When we traveled in the cattle cars, we didn't act with soldierly bearing. It's not like we were guarding the Tomb of the Unknowns at Arlington National Cemetery. It was more like kindergarten unleashed. As soon as we got in and sat on the steps, the floor, or the few available benches, the NCOIC (Non-Commissioned Officer in Charge) hollered, "Smoke 'em if you got 'em," and shut the doors. As we rumbled over rough dirt roads across the sprawling Fort Dix range complex, we erupted into raucous misbehavior inside the cattle car turned playpen. We poked fun at each other and joked around while some borrowed cigarettes, asked, "Got a light?" and smoked to their lungs' content.

"Hey Tony, how come you don't smoke? Don't you like us?" one soldier asked, and most of the boys laughed.

The pressure to join the group—to smoke like a rack of ribs in a meat locker, HaaKAACKing like my father before me—was almost too great to resist. Each trip to the ranges weakened my resolve to never smoke and strengthened my need to join the group. The longer I held to the oath I had sworn with Barbara, the more difficult it became to overcome the contempt I saw in the eyes of my fellow soldiers, who would not accept me until I made the leap over this cultural hurdle.

When the AMTRACS stopped, I couldn't get out fast enough. My eyes were watering and I could hardly breathe. We poured out with a great cloud of smoke, as if the cattle car were one giant tin lung, exhaling.

When we finished the day's training, we returned to the cattle cars and headed home. I knew I would be tested again, so I braced myself against the inevitable. Once we were inside, the NCOIC gave his blessing.

"Smoke 'em if you got 'em."

And so they did—thirty-five out of thirty-six of us.

"Hey Nauroth, why don't you become a real man today?" that same soldier taunted me. "Smoke with us."

He and a couple of his buddies gathered around me and blew smoke in my face. Closer, closer, closer, until there was no room for us cattle to move. I pushed away one of my dragon-breathing tormentors and muttered, "I'm wondering who the real man is here."

Before things got out of hand, a higher-ranking soldier shouted, "Knock it off! If he doesn't want to smoke, leave him alone!"

They backed down, but the senior soldier's intervention wasn't necessarily doing me any favors. Once again, I saw the contempt in the eyes of my compatriots, who in battle would expect me to fight with them as equals, together as a unit, cogs in the same wheel. They needed me to be a fellow they could completely trust, honor, and, especially, protect.

As the years rolled by, I had many opportunities to belong to various Army units; but in every case, I managed to resist their encouragement to smoke. I left the Army in 1995, only forty-five years old. Now, an Army veteran at seventy-two, I still see myself still as one unit with those men and women with whom I once served. And I never had to smoke to achieve that sense of belonging.

My mother wasn't so lucky. She was only sixty-seven on the day she died. For her, it wasn't just about smoking. Each cigarette was an extension of her personality, the way she would use it as an additional voice in our conversations by smacking it on the table before lighting up. Surprisingly, none of her six children ever smoked. And just like the Army, even though I never smoked, I still always felt like I belonged to my family.

***

Tony Nauroth is a retired US Army Master Sergeant who worked as a journalist with the Stars and Stripes newspaper in Germany when the Berlin Wall fell in 1989. Besides serving as Chief of Army Newspapers at the Pentagon, Tony's twenty-year career saw him reporting from throughout the United States, Europe, Central and South America, including Bolivia—the only place where he was ever shot at. They missed.

22

Lemonade

by Anne M. Bishop

As I step over and push around boxes in my new home, I realize I do not know where the dry goods or cleaning products are packed. My refrigerator arrives tomorrow, shelves need lining, dishes need unpacking and washing, and utensils need to make their way into the right drawers. My husband has left me in this mess to go on a business trip to California.

It has been a few days since the move from New Jersey to Maryland. Tears flow each day, brought on by the empty feeling of homesickness. When I think of the friends and family left behind, even more sadness fills my heart. I thought a new home, a new environment, and new experiences would fill me with joy. I had never considered it would make me feel like an outsider.

I grew up in New Jersey, attended college there, and raised my child near my childhood home. We lived in California and Virginia Beach off and on for a few years, but our home, family and friends were always waiting when out-of-state assignments ended. As I stand in my cluttered kitchen, thoughts float through years of childhood, marriage and motherhood spent in the comfort of the well-known. The sound of a truck pulls me back to the reality of all those boxes.

Finding a notepad and pen, I begin a shopping list. No patience to find the right box with the cleaning products. I need to move forward.

Safeway is a mile away and I need to escape the emptiness of this strange house. My two precious cats, Tabitha and Samantha, need food too. I quickly grab my purse and head out before the tears come.

The short list soon blossoms into a full page. My first trip to the store just the day before was for two items—I ran in and out. This is different. I stand at the automatic door, shopping list in hand, with a strange feeling of confusion. *Which aisle has the pet food? Where are the cleaning products?* New stores can be frustrating. I know I'll eventually find what I need, but for now I just have to deal with the muddling effects that moving has on the brain.

As I walk around the store reading the overhead signs, the aura of loss stays with me. I won't see a person I know here: no one to have a conversation with, to make plans for lunch or to ask if they are playing tennis tomorrow. No one to ask, "How's your mom?" or inquire about my family. No one knows me, no one knows I spent the last hour in tears, and no one cares.

Walking aisle by aisle, items I may have bought for company present another aspect of this change. Special items we always had on the shelf or in the freezer for unexpected guests. *Ah, I won't need any...no one is coming to the door.* Why fill my freezer with "guest" food when there is no prospect of visitors?

Nearing the checkout line with an overfilled cart, I think I see someone I know—then realize it's just my imagination, a look alike. I remind myself where I am: in a strange store in a small town that makes no promises.

Week followed week, the unpacking progressed. Bob returned home and we began to explore the smaller neighborhoods of Baltimore City. I found a position with a non-profit school and attended church, but a feeling of belonging eluded me for many years.

Perhaps the initial "welcome" from a neighbor gave me reason to feel as I did. With a tray of cookies, the woman came to my door in what seemed to be a welcome and possible offer of friendship. She refused my invitation to come inside, instead asking where I was from. She recommended that I meet people new to the area,

as born-and-raised Marylanders already had their social lives established. It made me feel about as unwelcome as possible. She moved
to a "better" neighborhood a few months later, and I never saw her
again.

Her "welcome" taught me to open myself to newcomers, be honest
about my feelings, and be thankful for those who had helped my
transition. After five long years, the yearning for "home" subsided,
tears faded and the house we lived in was no longer strange. I figured
out where items were in the store and, every once in a while, I saw
someone I knew shopping down the aisle or in the check-out line.

After settling in for twenty years, the experience began all over
again. This time, however, loneliness was more familiar to me: I had
already been a widow for twelve years. It wasn't any easier and it still
took time, but now I see all sides of belonging. Joining with a few
friends, no longer in need of an extended social circle. Enjoying art,
books and dinner out: activities as important as the family nearby.
Finding fulfillment in what I do for others closes that empty space that
occasionally gathers around my heart. I will probably never feel the
same sense of belonging as I did in my hometown, but one can make
lemonade out of lemons.

***

*Anne Bishop is a retired educator and director with a master's degree
in early childhood and postgraduate work in reading and administration. She returned to college after pursuing a career in banking. Anne
retired in 2013 to spend time with her grandsons, moving to California
in 2016 to enjoy their growing years. Three book clubs, two writing
groups, museums, gardens, theatre and volunteering fill Anne's days.*

23

From Spanish to English

by Camila Reimers

As the plane flew north, reality started to sink in. I looked at my three-month-old son sitting on my knees and promised him a better future than the one I was leaving behind. During the flight, I realized how much my life had changed: no more friends and family to share laughter and tears with, no more cold winter afternoons when all the women got together to change the world while knitting warm, fuzzy sweaters. Sitting high above the clouds, I said goodbye to summers filled with the smell of peaches and cherries, and the Andes Mountain whose presence followed me like a shadow.

When you say "September eleventh," most people think of the Twin Towers in New York. For me, that date is frozen in time in 1973 in Santiago, Chile, when military jets bombed the presidential palace, destroying the dreams of millions of Chileans hoping for a better world. Some of my friends died, others disappeared, and still others like me left the country for faraway places.

I was twenty-two years old at the time, studying education at the University of Chile in Santiago. After finishing my studies, I got married. My husband, a mining engineer, lost his job because he did not support the dictatorship that took over in 1973. For that reason, we immigrated to Venezuela in 1975 to begin a new life. From the first moment we landed in Caracas, I felt surrounded by solidarity and understanding from my new Venezuelan friends. My political participation was limited to intense discussions at friends' houses or in my own home—no more walks or public demonstrations. My two years under a dictatorship taught me not to express feelings and to accept the unacceptable.

After five years in Venezuela, and the birth of our second son, we left for Canada. My husband had a scholarship to earn his PhD at the University of British Columbia. From the minute we arrived in Canada in 1980, I fell in love with the mountains and forests of Vancouver. We lived at UBC Family Housing, where I met students from all the Canadian provinces and around the world. My younger son's best friend was from Ghana, and my eldest's best friend was from Newfoundland, Canada.

The houses were divided by size, depending on the number of children in each family. Families with two children lived on our street, those with one in high-rise buildings, and those with three on the street parallel to ours. To be surrounded by people with the same interests, surviving on meager scholarships and raising children, created an atmosphere of solidarity that reminded me of life in Chile, when friends and family were nearby.

Before I came to Canada, I was told people in this country were cold and distant, but my experience proved otherwise. When one of our neighbours finished her studies and returned home, my eyes were full of tears, and I missed her family as if we were old friends.

My husband finished his PhD and I my postgraduate studies in Language Arts. We moved to Montreal and then to Sudbury, Northern Ontario. Most people looked at me in disbelief and said, "Sudbury, you must be kidding!" On the contrary, this city was another wonderful experience. There I had my first opportunity to work in Canada. That job signaled the beginning of the second phase in my pursuit of a better world.

I worked with immigrants who wanted to return to their field of work. It gave me the opportunity to learn about the problems Canadian immigrants faced, particularly the struggle to find work. At first, I was convinced that the biggest barrier for immigrants was a lack of language skills. However, little by little I realized that the real obstacle was not believing in themselves, thinking they didn't have enough experience or weren't capable of passing an interview. For this reason, our team of teachers at the program decided to change our training methodology, giving participants the opportunity to show the skills buried in a "treasure chest" inside of them.

"If your English is excellent but you believe you are not capable, you won't get anywhere," we repeated day after day. A light of hope started showing in their eyes when they realized that their life experience—surviving a sea crossing in a small boat, experiencing grave fear and loss—gave them a richness of values as important as traditional work experience.

More than forty years have gone by since I left my country of origin. When I look at my eight grandchildren, I can say that Canada is my new home.

***

Originally from Chile, Camila Reimers has lived in Canada since 1980. She is a multidisciplinary artist presently engaged in textile arts, storytelling, and fiction writing. Camila is the author of five novels and numerous short stories in English and Spanish that have been published in Canada, Europe, and Latin America. Her writing has received several awards, including eight International Latino Book Awards.

24

Homeward Bound

by Bethia Sheean-Wallace

"A journey of a thousand Chinese miles starts beneath one's feet." – Lao Tzu

The sprawling home in the Hollywood Hills where I grew up had all the potential of a Shangri-La for myself and four older siblings. We had a mountain to explore with almost no parental restraints on our treks and adventures. Additionally, our Shangri-La was pretty isolated from our community. The unspoken rule in our home was *no visitors*. If you saw the condition of our mid-century ranch house, you'd know why. This rule began as circumstantial. While we never hosted birthday parties, close neighborhood buddies could venture into our rooms. Over the years, the rule was applied to just about everyone, all the time.

As the baby of the family whose older sibs—three brothers and a sister—were engaged in some unspoken competition to push me around, I certainly could have used a few visitors. Not to mention a community. We were a fiercely and unapologetically secluded family unit. As a result, we learned to comfort and nurture ourselves independently and developed all sorts of unhealthy ways to cope with our situation without discussion or counsel. We were lonely people in a lonely house.

I started literally walking away from home at a very early age. I was the kid who first walked off as a toddler, stirring up a lot of excitement involving police and knocking on neighbors' doors. I returned unscathed from who-knows-where, a tiny figure fearlessly wandering down the curvy narrow road.

By the time I was four, I was a common sight up and down Torreyson Drive where we lived. I wandered the neighborhood throughout the day—and I mean all day—from house to house. My friends' moms took me in without question. I pretty much adopted myself to a series of families throughout my childhood. Determined to avoid the chaos and negligence of my own home, I insinuated myself into these more well-tuned and orderly families. In many ways, I longed to belong to one of those families. I wanted to feel safe.

My preteen years saw this need to escape manifest in long distance expeditions. My dog Annie Rooney, an English pointer, always accompanied me on the long loop around the mountain or the hike down to Studio City. I'd walk miles down Mulholland and cross the freeway over the Cahuenga Pass Bridge to the Hollywood Reservoir. As a teen, I would ride off on my yellow Schwinn ten-speed and coast down the mountain to Hollywood or "The Valley" on the other side.

Fast forward twenty years to my life as a busy young mother of three, whose husband travels for a living. We had relocated to Florida. Looking back, clear signals of depression were all over the place. I created a new means of escape: drinking beer and smoking Camel Filters on the front porch. A nightly ritual. I hired babysitters so I could visit bars and drink in the good company of fellow alcoholics. The ill effects on my children were immeasurable. When I regained control, the outcome for myself and my family was improved; but the damage was done and the legacy of trauma established. To this day, we work together to identify and defuse the echoing disturbances of that time.

The good news is that I did quit my vices and started exercising, bit by bit. I took up running and joined a local running club. This is when I really entered the huge, diverse community of outdoor enthusiasts, and the fitness culture. My husband, Cleve, followed. Like all communities, it has its flaws—let's face it: *people* are involved. All in all, it is a great place to be. This is where you and your friends complete trail races, half-marathons, marathons, and triathlons. We all look up to the superhuman warriors who tackle ultra-marathons, century bike rides, and Ironman competitions. The sheer exhilaration and gratification of a long-distance run or ride has been a wonderful discovery for me. If running twenty-six miles isn't a nice, harmless way to satisfy a rambling instinct, I don't know what is.

The sense of belonging is empowering. According to people who should know, it is necessary for a decent quality of life. I did not grow up with a place of worship or even a social circle around the nucleus of my family. As an adult, I was folded into many associations through work, school, and my children, but the fitness community was one I sought out independently. I also think that without the improved health and self-confidence fitness has provided, I would not have involved myself in the more intimate, personally challenging, and enlightening community of writers—where we support, celebrate, and nurture one another.

That little girl who took off on literal and metaphorical journeys to find where she belonged still has a voice in the sixty-four year old woman I am now. The mother who sought solace in drinking and smoking—who seemed determined to proceed on a path of self-destruction—is there too, but she is not afraid anymore. She is not alone anymore. My odyssey continues, but the destination has changed. I am homeward bound. My journey is not just about me anymore. It is a course of growth and self-reflection, grace, and humanity. I know where I belong, and I am grateful for it.

***

Bethia Sheean-Wallace was born and raised in Los Angeles, married a Florida boy, and brought up three children with her husband in

Florida. Since then, the family has grown with the welcome addition of a daughter-in-law and a new baby granddaughter. Bethia has worked in library services for twenty years and has written over sixty Guided Autobiography essays.

Footsteps Bearing an Irish Tread

by Joanne Murphy Horn

G rowing up among extended family in the American Midwest, our summer lawns held footsteps of a long line of working-class immigrants from the ol' sod of Ireland.

My childhood was saturated with the sound of Gramma Susie's brogue and Mum's voice crooning the lullaby, "Toora Loora Loora," my memories punctuated by the sign of the cross at mealtimes and Mass. Our home was often populated with Irish cronies like Frank Tyrell, my father's best childhood buddy from St. Pat's school days, Sister Lucille, my mom's first cousin, and the rest of the clan on my mother's and father's sides.

In my twenties, walking the country lanes and city streets of Dublin, I saw my father's stocky stature again and again as farmers and urban dwellers went about their days. Many of the elderly sported the stark white hair, pink skin, and sky-blue eyes of my father. Growing up, my black hair, blue eyes and fair skin had been a bit unusual, but here in Ireland it was the norm. My brother Rich and I grew up seeing our father cross himself when he passed a church or tip his hat to the clergy on the streets of Chicago. Riding the buses in Dublin, I watched old gents tip their hats as my father had done. I noticed that making the sign of the cross was not reserved for church but was a commonplace gesture, repeated throughout my travels across the city and into the small villages of my cultural heritage. Amid the cool misty air of the Irish summer, it was clear that this was the culture and stock from which I'd come.

What, I wondered—besides my physical genetic traits and my Catholic upbringing—had been the impact of these Irish footsteps across my life path?

In the late 1940s, my father inherited forty acres of Wisconsin farmland from his grandfather, Richard Murphy. Richard had received this land grant when he arrived by covered wagon from Ireland via Ellis Island in 1848. I imagine my great-grandfather was dedicated to this farm, as the Irish were often relegated to mere tenants on farmland seized from their forebears by the English. And so "the Ole Forty," as we called it, was passed down from his children to his last remaining grandson nearly a hundred years later.

As a welcome escape from suburban life in Chicago, I spent childhood summers roaming those forty acres, tending my father's large vegetable garden, and riding horses with the neighboring farm kids. There, on the former soybean farm of my great-grandfather's family, I formed my first and most important connection to the earth.

Each season, Rich and I helped with the seeding, planting and harvesting of the tomatoes, greens, squash, and potatoes that comprised the taste of summer at the farm. We palnted hundreds of baby evergreens to create a forest grove behind the modest house my father had built the summer I turned six. Some afternoons I'd wander over to visit our neighbor, Mr. Schmidt, in his milking shed. Just as I rounded the doorway, he'd squirt me with warm milk right from the teat and give me a sip from the pail he was filling under Dolly's udder. Late each summer, just before we left the farm to return to school, Rich and I would spend hours collecting ripe hickory nuts strewn under the shade of the old tree's huge canopy.

All these experiences fostered within me the notion that owning and tending land was an important part of life.

I learned, as my father had learned when he was a boy working summers on his grandfather's farm, about stewardship. During our brief tenure on earth, we each have the opportunity to steward our lives, our property, and our families so that we might positively impact the people and property that outlast us. The joys of digging in the dirt, savoring the sweet taste of vine-ripened beefsteak tomatoes, and smelling the newly mown hay seeped into my being, lying dormant like seeds scattered by the autumn winds.

At thirty-nine, after living in most other regions of the United States, I finally made it to the Pacific Northwest. The climate was not unlike the one I experienced during multiple trips to Ireland.

While searching for a house in which to raise our young children, my husband and I wandered upon a run-down patch of three acres languishing in a desultory real estate market. Touring the house and property, I felt the seeds of my ancestral love of the land began to germinate and send out tendrils from somewhere deep and dark inside. I felt the tug of these acres: a couple of fruit trees, a pasture to raise a horse, a run-down outbuilding for a chicken coop, a large vegetable bed, and lawn space to play chase and build swings. This bit of farmland was a fit for me, an opportunity to tease sustenance and beauty from the land—just as my forefathers had.

Today, thirty-five years later, I'm still tending my wee patch of earth. Horses, dogs, and chickens have come and gone. Now the footsteps across my lawn are the tiny feet of grandchildren, running to pick blueberries and raspberries or stopping to watch bees suck nectar from the fruit of this land.

***

From 1987-2007, Joanne Murphy Horn provided conflict management services in Washington State through her consulting firm, Conflict Resolution Service, Inc. In 2009, she established Second Half Connections to provide educational forums in which participants explore their life journey. Joanne is working on a memoir and enjoys gardening, traveling, rug hooking and spending as much time as possible with her children and grandchildren.

26

Mystery and Wonder

by Gretchen Draper

Like many people, my true home is outside. I'm drawn to nature's mysteries and wonders—orchids the size of a fingernail in the bark of a black garlic tree and earthworms caught in the soil at the top of the tropical canopy, the call of the loon and the wind in the pines and the wren with fourteen voices.

This love of the world and its wild things sent me traveling over the years. It was there, in far-flung places, that I was met with the unexpected kinship of a stranger.

Years ago, my husband and I visited Cartago, a city in the central plateau of Costa Rica. It's a sacred place. Every August, thousands of pilgrims pay homage to La Negrita, the Black Madonna, a stone which holds the image of the Virgin Mary. La Negrita is the saint of healing, a holy relic. On her feast day, worshipers come for prayer, blessings and to give thanks for her special gifts.

She is enshrined in gold in the Basílica Nuestra Señora de los Ángeles.

The Basilica itself is a grand edifice, with hand-painted interiors, stained glass windows and ornate side chapels. I wandered through its magnificence and offered my own prayers to La Negrita. I was about to leave this gilded sanctuary through its massive entrance when a young Costa Rican woman smiled at me. She pointed to stone steps leading to a lower level of the building and gestured for me to come with her.

The air was cool as I followed her through a narrow, softly lit passageway. We came to a wide stone room with whitewashed walls and a hand-painted mural featuring a portrait of Juana Pereira, the young mestizo girl, who had discovered La Negrita in 1635.

The mural told the story in pictures, not words. It suited both of us, as I spoke little Spanish and the young woman little English. But that didn't stop our sharing. She swept her hands along the wall and explained the miracle in simple phrases.

The girl had been gathering firewood centuries ago when she discovered the doll-sized black stone sitting alone on a boulder. The small stone was etched with what seemed to be a woman's face. She took the stone home; but in the morning, it was gone. She searched and found that it had reappeared on the same boulder where she'd found it.

This happened three times. The girl carried the etched stone home but it always disappeared. Each time she found it again in the same place, on the same boulder.

The village priest declared the carving was the image of the Virgin Mary, and the villagers built a church over the huge rock.

And there it was—the boulder of the miracle—in this lower passage of the massive basilica. The young woman guided my hand and together we touched its cool surface.

She had more to show me. We entered a small room festooned with shiny metal charms. Cabinets stretched from floor to ceiling, overflowing with tiny silver and tin replicas of hands, limbs, heads, and hearts. One section held miniature cars, bicycles, wagons, horses, and an airplane. Another was filled with tokens representing people—old, young, babies, the sick and lame.

"Milagros," she whispered. Hundreds of tiny metal charms left by grateful worshipers, each representing a prayer of appreciation for the miracles granted in this sacred place. The gentle Costa Rican woman was sharing a deep part of her world with me, a stranger, in a manner so unlike the magnificence of the Basilica above.

Somehow, she had sensed I would best understand this miracle as it unfolded in the old passageway with its simple art, ancient rock and room with true symbols of peoples' faith.

We walked together back to the entrance and out into the hot Costa Rican afternoon. We spoke our names and said good-bye partly in Spanish, partly in English and with lots of laughter. I left full of gratitude and awe.

I had once considered these mysterious and wonderful experiences as solitary events. Yet as I retell my stories, the unexpected may start with one person, but it grows in depth and significance because we share our mysteries and wonder. The *sharing* is what transforms our experiences. We bond. We are surprised by what we have in common. We learn from one another. Our differences fade and our similarities multiply. We build trust in ourselves and in others. We begin to create a common story, a feeling of fellowship and a sense of belonging to something bigger than we ever imagined.

In the end, we all belong to this one beautiful and wildly imperfect world. I stand in wonder at the multitude of unknown shared experiences awaiting us all—you, me and the the open-hearted Costa Rican woman willing to share her miracles and faith with a stranger.

***

Gretchen Draper has been a writer, educator and traveler for the past fifty years. Currently, she is a Level II trainer in Kingian Nonviolence Conflict Resolution and a consultant with the National Writing Project in New Hampshire. Gretchen collaborates with her photographer/science teacher husband for peace and environmental justice.

27

The Web of Life

by Janet C. Constantinou

G rowing up in a family with one grandmother, two parents and three siblings, there were times when home was overbearing. A perfect escape was to wander the rolling hills of the Cotswolds behind our house with my beloved companion Jess, the family dog. As soon as I climbed high enough to look down on our house, I felt safe and free.

On sunny summer days, the tall grass and carpets of tiny wildflowers gave off a sweet scent that attracted buzzing bees and beautiful lady birds. I would stretch out on the warm grass and laze away the time, watching the passing clouds that created elaborate stories as they piled up in one spot and tumbled away elsewhere. There was always music in the hills—a distant cuckoo, a songbird nearby, the chirping of grasshoppers—with the occasional croaking frog rounding out the percussion.

I belonged to the warm earth, hidden by tall grass, filtered through the gauze of a spider's web, surrounded by the beauties of nature, forever fascinating and dynamic.

Idyllic as my childhood was, we all have to grow up. I fell in love and married a man whose skills were requisitioned in California. We left England the week after our wedding and took to the high seas on the Queen Mary, headed for New York. The threads that tethered me to my family in England began to stretch, growing more tenuous as time passed. Now I belonged to a Greek husband in a foreign land. This new belonging started out with great passion and excitement and we spent five adventure-filled years exploring the west coast of America on weekends and holidays. We drove to the tip of Baja California and even traveled south on the Mexican mainland to Mazatlán and as far north as Vancouver, Canada. Then, adding to the richness of our lives, a baby daughter arrived.

The inseparable bond with my husband was quite suddenly interrupted as a new bond was forged. A baby that we had talked about in the abstract was suddenly very present, needing to be fed, loved, and nurtured every moment of the day—a good part of the night. Focus was rapidly redirected. Dad took his work more seriously, feeling the weight of responsibility for the family, while I cut back on work to spend time with the baby. Our interests were suddenly so divergent: mine towards baby's needs and his towards graduate study and making ends meet. Overnight, my priority became this adorable, helpless bundle of joy. This new focus was, of course, shared by my husband; but the belonging I felt with every breastfeeding and diaper change became much more encompassing.

Within five years, my growing daughter had a little brother and once again the threads of bonding tugged us in new directions. The children stimulated new friendships with families similar to our own. Visits to the beach, meetings at the sand pit, swim practice and competitions, birthday parties, and school events brought us close to families with similar interests. We developed numerous loose bonds of expediency: supporting childhood friendships, facilitating carpools and attending meets. My web became very large, with a tight center of family members and loose threads stretching in all directions. Perhaps it was a time when bonds were taken for granted, there were so many: work colleagues, teachers, coaches, tutors, and the parents of our children's friends with whom we coordinated gatherings, transportation, sleepovers and camping trips.

Meanwhile, our own family bonds were tugged hither and thither. Largely influenced by external events, they swayed from very tight to distressingly loose as circumstances and friendships oscillated. Then, though it seemed like a flash, the children were planning for college and leaving home. Our bonds turned to tatters as a gap year took one traveling around the world, their plans shared with us more often after the fact than before. There was a period when my strongest bond was with the mailbox. The letters from my mother, quickly scanned between bills and advertisements, now took on greater significance. News of aging relatives passing on caused me to treasure her letters and the memories they evoked. Then there was the excitement of sporadic letters from our children: unpredictable, sometimes very scant and other times rich with experiences. Occasionally, these missives transmitted the feeling that we were missed, but they were often news of a life from which we were totally separate.

The arrival of grandchildren started to reshape the web. There was a renewed closeness as our grown children recognized patterns in their behavior that mirrored those seen in their own parents. But time raced on and the web again started to unravel. Strands became long and tattered, many severed as family members leave this world. Weaving and unraveling all over again.

Gradually, I have rediscovered that our bond with the earth is the only one that lasts forever, beautifully and patiently awaiting our return.

***

Janet C. Constantinou was born in the Cotswolds of England in 1942. She is married and has a daughter, son, and two grandchildren. After completing nursing training at Oxford in 1962, Janet worked in medical research at Stanford Medical Center for over thirty years. She completed a PhD in Infant Development in 2002. In retirement, Janet serves as a volunteer docent at the Asian Art Museum in San Francisco, California.

28

Rotating At Lunch

by Jana Rae Corpuz

I t was my first party. I entered a house full of unsupervised teens running rampant through of a mess of red cups, chip bowls, scattered shoes and blaring music. Somehow, I ended up watching a classmate take apart a pen and discard the ink and cap while another person folded up a piece of foil lengthwise. Some crushed white substance was sprinkled onto what looked like a mini foil trough, while another person held a lighter underneath the foil. Smoke began to slowly rise, and the person holding the hollow pen brought it to his lips and inhaled the thick smoke.

I was intrigued.

Being fifteen felt rough. I was never comfortable in my skin. I always felt like an outsider looking in. Other girls seemed to know how to act, what to wear, and how to do their make-up. In Catholic school, most girls wore plaid skirts paired with pristinely ironed white button-down shirts. I wore stiff navy pants and wrinkled polo shirts. Something about me was different. I moved through the world feeling awkward and unsure—like an alien from outer space.

Feeling like I couldn't fit in anywhere, I tried to fit in everywhere. At lunch, I would rotate where I sat. First, I would spend time with my childhood friends. Though we had common interests, it still seemed like something was missing. After a few minutes of catching up and eating, I'd make my way to hang out with my wrestling teammates. You would think I'd find camaraderie on a sports team, but I was a girl on the all-boys team. After the jocks, I'd then hang with the Filipino people. They looked the most like me.

Despite my strategy, I still felt completely alone. It was a deep sadness, empty and bottomless, at times unbearable.

Growing up in the 90s, the "Just Say No," campaign was drilled into our heads. At yearly lectures and presentations in student assembly, they warned of the dire dangers of drugs, but never told how it would feel or how it could help.

As I watched the pen and foil science experiment, in awe of something so foreign to me, the pen was suddenly passed my way. I grabbed it without hesitation and inhaled. What followed was several hours of methamphetamine-induced rapid speech and newfound friends. I suddenly felt connected to others, something I hadn't felt before. It was the first time I actually felt like part of something.

I chased that feeling for the next eighteen years, but never really felt it again.

Instead, things got worse. Feelings got worse—depression, anxiety, mood swings. One day I found myself in front of a bunch of pills with a large bottle of whiskey.

I was thirty-three and I was done.

It was a lifetime of wandering, college, career changes, a master's degree, several failed relationships, travel, marriage, deaths. My life felt just like my high school lunch rotation. Doing all the things, hanging with all the people, but never really fitting in.

After hours of sobbing, drinking, a couple pills, and googling best ways to kill yourself, I had a solid plan to die—I just couldn't go through with it.

Instead, I decided to get help. I checked myself into the hospital and was directed to Alcoholics Anonymous.

I walked into my first meeting, terrified. I couldn't look anyone in the eye. I kept my head low, shrinking with shame, as if everyone knew about the suicide attempt that for some reason made me feel like a failure.

To my surprise, most of the people looked happy. They talked and shared everything they were feeling.

I sat in the back. I heard things that I painfully related to. For the entire hour, I rode waves of emotions, listening, hearing pieces of myself in each story, yet staying silent.

I cried at every meeting. Day after day, I bolted at the end instead of staying to visit afterward, embarrassed by my own existence.

Something happens when you get sober. The feelings that you drank to avoid finally come to the surface, and there is no way to numb them. Feelings that became so uncomfortable, I couldn't stay quiet any longer.

I raised my hand to share. Tears streamed down my face as I kept my head down and blurted out, "I feel like shit even though I am sixty days sober." I paused reluctantly, "I am sober, and I still feel like I want to die."

A roar of laughter erupted. The crowd applauded. The mere shock of their reaction forced me to finally look up from the floor. I was met with welcoming warmth in people's eyes. Heads nodded as they gently smiled at me. The laughs, nods, and smiles were filled with genuine, loving understanding. Never in my life had I felt so understood. In that moment, the comfort of their empathy melted away my pain. I was forever changed.

People talked to me afterward, and this time I stuck around. I continued attending meetings and got to know other sober women. I connected with them, and they loved me unconditionally.

I finally felt like part of something—like I had a place to go, a place where I was welcome.

I've spent much of my life jumping from one thing to the next, rotating at lunch, trying to be someone I am not.

In AA, I learned that I don't have to rotate. Not only do I belong to the group, I belong in the world. I deserve to be here and I am enough. So I'm going to stay in one place and just be me.

***

Jana Rae Corpuz is a writer, artist, and licensed marriage and family therapist from Los Angeles, California. A former journalist, she now works with trauma survivors. Jana writes stories about her experiences in mental health and substance abuse recovery, surviving trauma and growing up as a second generation Filipino.

29

A Warm Bath

by Annie Lion

I was adopted at birth. My adopted family consisted of my mother, father, and sister, Amy. My parents provided well for me academically, financially, and physically. They shaped the core values that define me today. Yet, for reasons I am still gnawing on, I did not feel part of them at a deeper level. My differences from them were questioned and judged. They saw me as a person of average abilities, short-tempered, high-strung, disobedient, rude, spoiled, and generally too high a risk taker for their comfort. I recall my mother saying on numerous occasions that she doubted I would live to see twenty years of age. Granted, many of these labels fit: I regularly climbed out of windows just to hang out on a tiled roof or wandered away in public settings, causing a panic. Meanwhile, Amy clung closely to our mother's skirt. I'm still not sure what I was running from during those early years.

My father used to say that I ran away from home as soon as I could walk. At four years old, I already had strong best friends (and in later years, boyfriends) with whom I spent as much time as possible. Usually, my friends had families in which I enmeshed myself. Their families included me in meals, outings, and vacations. Most weekends throughout junior and high school were spent at girlfriends' houses. In my early teen years, I recall dozens of weekend and summer vacations with my friend Susie. With six children, her family always provided a boisterous cacophony of pranks, horseback riding, bawdy songs, and stolen moments for cigarettes or Cuba-Libres. Her older brother named his first child after me.

My high school boyfriend, Lee, wove me into his family for years. I was invited to countless weekday and weekend suppers. I loved spending hours with his mother, a therapist. She and I remained strong friends long after my romantic relationship with Lee ended.

I became even closer to my college boyfriend Rick's family. His mother Anna, who was also a therapist, once said I was the daughter she never had. She taught me to make Polish dishes: pierogi, stuffed cabbage, gefilte fish and others. She sewed me lovely dresses from scratch and was always generous. For several years, we ate Sunday brunch together, played tennis in the afternoon, cooked a simple dinner, and competed in Scrabble. Anna would then pack us off with leftovers for the week. She and I remained close until her death, years after both Rick and I had married other people.

In my late twenties, I married Tito, whose family had been friends with mine since I was six. I had attended both his sisters' weddings, so dating their brother was a no-brainer. His parents had the best marriage I had ever seen: they cooked healthy meals, read, watched Masterpiece Theatre, gardened, and exercised together. When each wanted to return to school for graduate degrees in their forties, they fully supported the other and grew together as a couple. They showed affection, respect, and delight in each other. I admired them from a very early age, and was thrilled to become a member of a loving, supportive, and accepting family. His mother, Peggie (also a therapist), subtly and assuredly provided guidance and support as I entered motherhood. She even took birth coaching with me in case Tito did not make it back from work for the birth. When one of our daughters needed specialized infant care, she researched the specialists, made the appointments, and took me to them. We still remain close, even though her son and I became uncoupled fourteen years ago.

I felt like I belonged in each of these families over the decades. Yet the puzzle pieces that compose my soul still felt incomplete.

A true sense of belonging has been a life-long pursuit, frequently met through non-family members until recently. A year ago, I found three sisters from my birth mother's side. I knew they existed and had tried to contact our birth mother several times over the decades, with resounding and resolute rejection. After her death, genetic testing connected me to a first cousin, who connected me with my three birth sisters. They were shocked and devastated. How could their mother have hidden my existence all their lives? They are still replaying conversations and lifelong experiences with their mother, trying to square the new reality with the past one. Yet they welcomed me with open hearts and couldn't wait to know and fully integrate me into their lives.

Over the past year, we have visited six times. I talk with each of them weekly. We share a cutting sense of humor, red-hot irreverence, wicked loyalty, self-deprecation, and love for each other. We all enjoy a good deal and a delicious grudge. In certain phrases or glimpses of physical attributes, I hear or see myself in them.

At sixty-six, I finally know how it feels to have utter loyalty, acceptance, and awe of the full battery of my flaws and gifts. And, on occasion, appreciation for my irreverent or rule-challenging sides. Like a warm, calm, deep bath, my newfound sense of belonging provides safety from hurts, and acceptance of who I am.

***

Ann Lion spent her career working in global public health. Once retired with her husband on a mountain in rural West Virginia, she started taking memoir writing classes online during the pandemic. This is one of the stories Ann has written for her one-year-old granddaughter.

30

Get Out Of Your Own Way

by Patricia O'Neill

The notion of belonging is complex. Is it a basic human trait, born out of a need to live in groups for protection? Does it derive from a need for love? Is it necessarily linked to our self-esteem? Is it so essential to our well-being that when we cannot achieve it, we are driven to despair? I have periodically pondered these questions in my lifelong approach to (and avoidance of) belonging.

One thing I believe: the relationship is set early on. As philosopher Miguel Ruiz suggested in "The Four Agreements," even as infants and toddlers we receive subtle messages from our parents that we internalize and then judge ourselves by. My internalized message—constantly reinforced at home—was that nothing I did was ever good enough. I carried this with me throughout my young life, lacking confidence or belief in myself. I was the neighborhood kid everyone picked on. In school I was always an outsider, longing to be part of the "in" group but being endlessly rejected.

Life began to turn around in college, but by then my negative self-image was firmly fixed. Regardless of how much I achieved, I could never acknowledge it or feel it was good enough. By extension, I also believed everyone I met was better than me. I continued to judge myself, striving to be perfect so I would be accepted and always falling short.

Fortuitously, at this time, I began to experience flashes of insight that suggested my self-perceptions were not entirely accurate. Nonetheless, this pattern of insecurity was not finished with me.

As I became successful, in a pathetic attempt to overcome my self-imposed "outsiderness", I squandered absurd amounts of money trying to create a physical image that would draw people to me. I now know I had it all backward. The person I became on the outside bore no resemblance to the person on the inside. Worse, I did not like this person. I became more detached and began to realize that (1) I had been trying so hard to fit in, I did not know who I was; and (2) I did not particularly care about fitting in with my peer group.

Eventually, I learned to enjoy my own company, which was the first baby step toward belonging. Before I could go further, however, I had to get out of my own way.

In hindsight I believe that "outsiderness" breeds a particular form of self-centeredness. At least it did in my case. I needed to look at it.

One manifestation of my self-centeredness was that I was really angry. In this regard, I was also really lucky. Serendipitously, on a solo trip to India I stumbled onto Buddhism, which set me on a path to substantially mitigating my underlying resentment at feeling rejected and changing my heart.

Nonetheless, I found new ways to sabotage myself, abusing food and drink to escape my pain and loneliness. In that case, cancer intervened, demonstrating the futility of such self-destructive behavior. From this I not only learned to take better care of my body but to love the outdoors and walking.

Yet, I still had more lessons to learn. Several times, I experienced the loss of "things" that I used to think were important, and the loss of people and creatures I loved—who really *were* important. Understanding the true meaning of loss was life changing.

While sorting all this out, I was extremely fortunate to be traveling the world, meeting people of diverse cultures, ethnicities, and socio-economic levels. These contacts opened my eyes to a new dimension and profoundly changed me. I saw that many people in the world, even in developed countries, never have the material things we in America take for granted. It is worse in developing countries, with many people lacking access to adequate food, shelter, and medicine. I became enormously grateful for the abundant blessings in my life and, at the same time, deeply upset by the injustice so many suffer. Along the way I made many lifelong friends and learned how wonderful people can be, regardless of their circumstances.

All of this boundlessly broadened my perspective and further opened my heart. I learned to listen to my heart, and subsequently I have always known where I belong and with whom. If you pay attention, you can feel it. It is just that simple.

As I became comfortable in my own skin, I learned a few more things. The first is that attitude is everything. How you view the world and your circumstances is far more important than the circumstances themselves. Second, it is healthy to be honest with yourself and accept yourself as a whole person with flaws. Third, helping others become their best selves is infinitely more fulfilling than worrying about what others think of you. Fourth, setting goals and never giving up on them is exciting and life-giving. Finally, compassion is absolutely fundamental to life and happiness; and trusting the universe is a source of peace.

For me, all these truths establish the foundation for belonging. Belonging is first and foremost about love. Then it is about accepting yourself, identifying your core beliefs, values, and principles and learning how to live by them. Finding purposeful work you are passionate about is also hugely fulfilling, especially if it is helpful to others. If you are open to new experiences, this too is joyful. The rest will take care of itself. I really believe that.

***

Dr. Patricia O'Neill is a social gerontologist and attorney whose research interests are focused on ageing in China, Italian culture, and self-help. She is the author of Urban Chinese Daughters: Navigating

New Roles, Status, and Filial Obligations in a Transitioning Culture *(Palgrave-MacMillan, 2018) plus several articles and book chapters.*

31

The Value of Exploration

by Anna Wallace

M addie, my friend's daughter, was drafting her application for an Antarctic Young Explorers programme in which she was asked to explain why exploration was important in the 21st century. In helping to prompt her, my mind skydived back to the years I spent navigating between dots on the globe. I waxed lyrical for a few minutes, losing her after about twelve seconds. In that moment a door to memory lane creaked ajar, one that hadn't been opened for years. As guided autobiography has taught us, you must honour your story by peeking behind that cobwebbed door.

Starting in my early twenties, I spent a decade observing new cultures. I met scores of new people, tried new things, adapted to new customs, and found out what I was made of when stripped of the familial structures and familiar comforts of my youth. I worked a stint in cosmopolitan Australia, pottered around Southeast Asia, and did the expat thing in London while doing the city break thing in Europe. Coming back to see loved ones in New Zealand every few years meant more stopovers in Asian cities, a trip to the Cook Islands and exposure to California.

Travelling may seem like the opposite of belonging. And at the time, it did feel like I was running away from a stifled existence. When you disembark from the universal surrounds of planes at an international airport, everything is different. You most certainly do not feel like you belong. It's an exhilarating, jarring journey away from the known. You're surrounded by strangers and sometimes don't have a place to stay. The language can be foreign, as can the food, currency and culture. There are animals you've never seen, ethnicities you've never encountered, and new dangers to navigate.

When everything is different, you cling to commonalities and connections.

A mega-watt smile seen across the room at my first overseas job lifted my spirits (even becoming a romantic interest for a short while). Helpful advice in a scary new land lightened our backpacker load. Jokes over nuanced accents never got old (why is it I struggled so with the Scottish brogue?). A trek in the northern Thai jungle, a boat trip in Laos and a Vietnam War odyssey were unifying and edifying experiences—the ride back always more talkative, with formalities shattered by special moments shared. Talking with a Thai prostitute, visiting a sex show in Amsterdam, helping homeless people in London. Exploring Chinatowns around the world, Mardi Gras, music festivals—eyes wide open. Bonding over food likes and dislikes ("Don't order a hot 'dog' whatever you do," "Which curry can we stomach tonight?", "What snacks from home are you missing?"). Becoming fast friends by joining a sports team, drinking with teammates, and then raising our kids together.

Tokens remain: Swiss friends met in Asia visited us in England and I still have the tea and coffee canisters they bought me from Camden Market. Seventeen years later, we are still friends on Facebook.

On a flight from Bangkok to London, I was feeling unsure about leaving carefree backpacking behind to establish my adult life. But then I started talking to the older gentleman on my left. He'd been in Thailand for his daughter's wedding—"marvelous!" He said that his wife was no longer of this world—"oh no!" But she was the one who encouraged them to travel and enjoy life as a family, while this gentleman thought they should use the money to become more financially secure. "I'm so glad that we lived her way," he said. When she was dying of breast cancer, they agreed that exploring had provided such treasured, worthwhile memories.

In all those moments, I connected with other humans like me! They may have only been part of my tribe for a few hours or a few days; but finding others with the same sense of curiosity and empathy , a desire to see new things, was a joyous feeling.

Now, after raising a child, failed relationships, houses bought and sold, a career of sorts, and friendships come and gone, there is only me and my reflection in the morning mirror. Someday when you have these wrinkles and dimples, will you have lived out of your comfort zone, explored who you really are beneath? Leaving the nest fearful but keen is how we test our mettle and inform our identity; it's part of the tool kit of life experience that brings about new perspectives. And that is something to be proud of.

Maddie won't understand this yet. Hopefully, she will one day. With my son Rylan having just started high school, I coach him to "find your tribe." I don't want him to anguish over the teenage feelings of not belonging—not when there are so many good times ahead.

I may no longer be an active traveler of far-off lands, but I feel a heady glow every time there's a shared connection: a common hobby, a smile exchanged, a new friendship ignited, a mutual fear overcome. I seek out truth and compassion, an open heart and lived wisdom. Memoir writing gives you all these things. Exploration gives you all these things. And both have helped me feel a sense of belonging in who I am and what I have to offer.

***

Anna Wallace has always loved stories, particularly oral history and personal life story. After a twenty-year career in marketing and communications, she's returning to this passion through guided autobiography. Anna likes to watch movies, read memoirs, play sports, socialise with friends, and explore with her son (and dog) in Christchurch, New Zealand.

Part | THREE

Creating Belonging Where We Land

32

The Glove That Fits

by Liz Dossa

A s I drove the curving inner road on campus, sunlight gilds the white skin of the eucalyptus above me. A gaggle of plaid-skirted girls walk down the hill, laughing. Quiet filters through the oaks, down the ivy-covered hill, across the meadow.

I first came to Burlingame on a morning like this in 1979 to interview for a part-time teaching job at a school run by the Sisters of Mercy. I knew nothing about women of religion, but wanted to teach again. I drove behind the school and parked in one of the faculty spots. Unsure of where to go, I rang the bell at the top of the stairs.

A year before, I had taught where I didn't belong. A friend found me a job at an elite girls' school—a strange setting for me as a public school kid. Even in their uniforms, the girls breathed privilege: BMWs in the parking lot, housekeepers, birthday parties on the lawns of imposing homes. None of it felt comfortable, and I wasn't a dynamic teacher. I didn't really fit.

At the end of the semester, the head mistress brought me into her walnut-paneled office to say they wouldn't need me next year. Her message was diplomatic but clear.

That dismissal led to the rest of my life.

I waited at the huge oak door of another imposing brick mansion surrounded by oaks. I had no idea who the Sisters of Mercy were. I had not grown up Catholic and had no preconceived ideas about nuns with rulers in the classroom. But what if I didn't belong here either?

Sister Janet brought me into an office overlooking the driveway. She was a small woman in a simple blue dress with a white head covering, which I later learned was a "coif." There were no long, flowing robes or beads around her waist. The Sisters of Mercy had taken steps into the twentieth century. She asked me questions: Where had I taught? Why did I want to teach here?

No theology was required to teach English. I jumped at the chance to teach a couple of classes.

Soon, I found myself squished into a small closet-like office with three women, creating lesson plans for freshmen—how to make adverbs fun, ways to introduce and discuss The Scarlet Letter. I loved it all: the interchange, the sharing of ideas, the encouragement.

Years later, a job opened up with the Sisters themselves. Even after being on the campus for a number of years, I had no idea that the Sisters who lived in the convent down the hill were the real power brokers. They had founded and now ran the school from a distance. I knew one or two Sisters, but the idea that a community of women could pull their power together to choose their own destiny was new to me.

For the interview, three of us sat in a large conference room with a blackboard and a few chairs. Sister Joan Marie asked about my past on the campus, glancing down at the questions on her papers. She was a thin, quick woman with a flashing smile.

A few days later, she called and offered me a full-time position in communications. Hearing the offer was a dizzying experience and a turning point in my life. This was more than a job. It was an invitation to know them, to help them speak to each other and to outsiders. Looking back, it was as though I found a glove that fit my hand and slipped right into it.

The Sisters, like most women, liked to talk to each other. They were drawn together by consulting and consensus. Each had chosen to be part of a group with a shared vision. Not a gaggle of geese kvetching and preening, but a team pulling together—and stopping to discuss the direction along the way. Why, then, did they need a communications director?

Women religious prize communication among themselves and with the external public. Communication is necessary for community. The job was an important one to the Sisters, and most women religious were finding that it was necessary to hire lay people to help them with this function. I was going to be part of discussions around that table, creating newsletters, sharing laughter in the lunchroom.

As a staff member, this is where I learned what "belonging" requires in the long run. There are rules, commitments made to the purposes of the community: to the poor, the sick, and the uneducated, as their founder outlined. A sense that what you do—from demonstrating against unfair housing practices to driving a hybrid car—is part of belonging. Your actions reflect on your community.

I've been part of the Sisters' lay staff for twenty-five years. I attended the general meetings when Sister Agatha stood and vigorously defended her proposed safe house for women leaving prison. They didn't all agree. Some thought it was too risky. Others said Agatha had lots of ideas and didn't always stick with them. (The Sisters compromised by accepting another Catholic social service organization as the major sponsor of the safe house. That worked well, and the house has flourished over the years.)

For over two decades, I've mourned with them through the passing of coworkers and family members. The community shrinks year by year. Aging together is a part of the package of belonging together.

Belonging on this campus means knowing all the paths, dirt and paved, seeing the way the light gilds the white skin of the eucalyptus along the inner road, knowing there are limits. I'm still an outsider, but a helpful and committed one.

At this moment, I belong here. That belonging has sheltered and nurtured me for most of my adult years. I reflect on how essential that sense is, how lucky we are to find it—even temporarily—in a classroom, a regular spot in a coffee shop, a pew, or an office desk. Belonging is a gift.

***

Liz Dossa has a lifelong fascination with people's life stories. She is a communication professional for the Sisters of Mercy and former high school English teacher. Liz is also a certified Guided Autobiography instructor who has led classes and retreats at Mercy Center, Foster City Recreation Department, and the Foster City Library.

33

The Salad Bowl

by Sandy Cook

On a hot summer day in 1977, in my battered old Alfa Romeo with no air conditioning, I sweated through the one-hour commute from ritzy Encino to my home in sleepy Simi Valley, California. I wasn't going straight home tonight because I was donating blood at St. Rose of Lima Catholic Church. At least it would be air conditioned. While waiting, I cooled my heels and other body parts until a resounding voice called out, "Sandra Goldstein." I felt an extra whoosh of air as all heads swiftly pivoted in my direction, eyes following my walk to the table. I could only assume the turning heads and curious stares were directed at my very Jewish name in a Catholic Church. Funny how there had been no reaction when I went to a Jewish temple with my husband. Everyone there assumed I was Jewish, not a shiksa. Where did I belong? Was my previous identity as Irish American Catholic void because my name no longer matched?

Growing up in small town Clarkston, Washington, there was not much diversity. In 1970, when I moved on to New York, Washington, D.C. and the Los Angeles area, I saw people quickly categorized by visual clues. With dark hair, dark eyes and fair skin, I was often claimed by cultures whose coloring resembled mine. What a gift that turned out to be! For a brief time, I got to be Italian, Greek, Mexican, Puerto Rican, French, and—despite my fair skin—even African American.

The funniest example of my mistaken identity took place in a pub in Ireland. It was 1989, and a group of bicycle racers dressed in costumes

were slaking their thirst and looking for mischief. My sister Debbie
sent me to the bar to get us each a Guinness. A short man (dressed in
baby doll pajamas with a pacifier around his neck) chastised me for
ordering a jar instead of a pint, "Ladies don't drink jars!" He grabbed
my wrist and began twirling me with great abandon. I thought I might
spin out the door or into the laps of strangers. All the while I mouthed
"HELP!" to my sister and her newfound Irish friends, whose only
answer was howling laughter. As I gasped for air, my new pajama-clad
friend dragged me back to the bar, hollering, "Why don't you talk?
I see you on TV and you never shut up." I asked who he thought I
was. He replied, "You know who you are, you, you Oprah Winifred!"
I couldn't believe it. Just as the music stopped, I corrected him at the
top of my lungs, "I'm not Black!" Even visiting my mother's homeland,
they clearly didn't view me as one of them.

After my name became Goldstein, of course, I was always believed
to be Jewish. Even after Jews learned that I was not truly part of
their clan, their welcome lived on. They didn't focus on their error
of assumption, but on the feelings we shared.

In 1993, when I was substitute teaching in a predominantly Mexican
school in Longmont, Colorado, an impish twelve-year-old boy stared
at me all day. Sidling up to the teacher's desk, he asked where I was
from. I told him I had moved here from California. He shook his head
and giggled, saying, "But you are..."

"What?" I asked.

He insisted, "You know you are."

After a couple more rounds of this, he declared, "Mex!" I laughed
and explained my Irish heritage, but he wasn't buying it. He thought I
was trying to pass. Nevertheless, the Hispanic kids treated me as one
of them every time I subbed at their school.

In another classroom, a student referenced the American Melting
Pot in a heated discussion. Another student took exception with the
term, as only a passionate teenager can reject a label they don't
choose. I understood their objection that ingredients melting together
lost their original identity. I suggested that we might be more like

a giant salad bowl, where individual ingredients retain their original form and flavor but complement each other, and there is no limit to the number of ingredients. We laughed together and adopted the salad bowl metaphor for our country.

We were different from each other, but we belonged together.

My acceptance into groups for which I have no legitimate claim has reinforced my lifelong belief that *all people crave acceptance, not just tolerance.*

The only way I know to navigate differences in a salad is to approach its ingredients openly, sincerely, and with no hidden agenda. Think the best of others and they will generally give you their best. Keep your expectations high. If results fall short, try to figure out why by mutual discussion. Explore assumptions and exceptions from all sides.

This may sound overly simplistic, but it works for me. My family includes Jews, Christians, Agnostics, Far Eastern religions, Mexican Americans, African Americans, Native Americans, European Americans. We do not pretend differences do not exist. We embrace our differences and each other with love, pride, and loyalty. Our salad is unique with a perfect blend of distinct flavors.

***

Sandy Cook is a retired English teacher. In addition to teaching in three states, she worked in the business world in New York, Washington, D.C., and California. Sandy and her husband live in Colorado and together have six children, fourteen grandchildren and four great-grandchildren.

34

Home Is Where The Memories Are

by Terry Northcutt

Whirlwind romances are exciting, heady, exhilarating. Two strangers see each other across a crowded room. There is chemistry, there is attraction, there is passion. At first glance, they know they are soulmates. They belong together. Forever.

Two years ago, I had the same intoxicating experience with a place. Specifically, a town just outside of Hartford, Connecticut. I was head over heels in love with the place. And I wanted to move there. Forever. Until death do us part.

This romance wouldn't have happened if I hadn't been a bit low and vulnerable at the time. It started with friends planning the next stages of their lives. They talked about moving closer to children, dreamed of warmer climates, they considered second careers and retirement communities with resort-style amenities. Soon, they were gone. And they didn't move just a few miles away from our Maryland home; they moved hundreds and hundreds of miles away.

One day when walking Gracie, my goldendoodle, I realized not one friend lived close enough for a weekend outing where we might create memories to weave through future conversations that will begin with "Remember when we...", "Remember how you...", "Remember when I..." And this thought led to another realization: the decades-long relationships that had supported and nurtured me and brought me great joy might not be sustainable over such distance. Email and phone conversations maintained a degree of connection, but would that be enough over time?

As this loss and question ballooned into awareness, I grew certain it was time for my husband and I to move. There was nothing and no one tying us to Maryland. I decided we should move to a place closer to friends, with a lower cost of living and four seasons (just slightly warmer than Maryland in the winter). In other words, I decided to treat my loss as a problem to be solved. Soon, my husband and I were taking short vacations to places where we might want to live. I worked remotely, so Gracie and I joined my husband on his consulting trips.

After weekends of exploring, we soon found a strong possibility for a place we could call home. We were scheduled to stay for six months in Connecticut for one of my husband's consulting jobs. Within six weeks, we discovered the area had a river park where I could run my dog and nurture my soul, a ballroom dance studio where the creative staff thrived on entertaining theme nights and showcases, a library filled with avid and insightful readers, spring festivals, and a committed writing group. Delighted with the lifestyle that was evolving and the wonderful people we were meeting, we contemplated moving to this charming place. Forever. It was indeed an exciting, heady, and exhilarating experience.

By spring we would have searched for a house. But in March, the pandemic forced us home. My husband was to work remotely for the remaining months. The enchantment of a whirlwind romance is powerful, and the abrupt end to our Connecticut romance left us feeling disappointed. Once we settled back into our home, we scoured the internet for a house and researched moving costs. Unfortunately, our research revealed more than we wanted to know. Facts quickly banished the enchantment and shattered our delusions. In the Nutmeg State, both sales and property taxes were higher than in Maryland. There were more days below freezing, twice the snowfall, and no reciprocity enabling me to retain my psychologist license between the states. And while we had acquired a cast of wonderful acquaintances, we were still far from our close friends. Infatuation, created by loss, suddenly crashed on the hard rocks of reality.

Sobered by these facts and unable to renew our search for somewhere else to move during the pandemic, I focused on walking. Each day as I walked my dog to the farm or the river, my mind drifted amidst the colors of the season, the sight of ospreys soaring over the river, deer fleeing with their short tails flashing white, and squirrels chasing each other in spirals around tall trees. These had become as much a part of me as the relationships that had spanned decades. Even the sounds of the seasons had become a part of me. I knew that spring brought the silvery bells of the spring peepers, the duck-like cackling of the wood frog, the trill of the toad, and the mating calls of the birds. Late summer brought the crescendo and decrescendo of buzzing and chattering insects, autumn the honking of geese and chirping of crickets, and winter a silent stillness interrupted only by the occasional magic of snow and the caw, caw, caw of the crow.

As memories of sights and sounds accumulated like old friends, I realized what a quiet, deep connection I had forged with the place I had lived my entire life.

This was where I belonged. Forever. Until death do us part.

Our time in Connecticut was exhilarating, but it would be years before it became part of me, years before the sights and sounds of the seasons became part of me, years before I belonged. While grieving what had been, I knew I needed a place made of memories associated with old, cherished friends that along with phone conversations assured me that our bond would continue over time and distance. I also knew I needed a place to support and nurture me through the hard work of forging new friendships and creating new memories that began with "Remember when we...", "Remember how you...", Remember when I..."

***

Terry Northcutt is a Guided Autobiography Instructor who works one-on-one with people of all ages to help write their life stories. She is currently pursuing certification as a Book Coach to help writers craft and complete novels, memoirs, and nonfiction.

35

A Constant Thread

by Dana Curtin

Homosexuality was still a crime in 1965, when I fell in love with another girl at the age of eighteen. I felt I had lost my sense of belonging forever. Ever since, I have suffered from a sad internal story, often forgetting my successes and joys. Though it took more than fifty years to realize, I can finally reclaim the whole story: despite believing I was separate, I have always belonged.

Growing up in the baby booming San Fernando Valley after WWII, my young family was one of many beginning new life chapters. My parents, two brothers, and I lived just a Sunday drive away from grandparents. The newly built First Christian Church of North Hollywood was the center of our family life. Even if I hated getting dressed up for church every Sunday, even if my best friend and I giggled irreverently in our pew, even if I was our family's redheaded wild child, I was devoted to God. I prayed every night that Jesus might speak to me.

Like all my friends, I wanted to marry a handsome, wonderful man, raise a family in the church and grow old with my husband and grandchildren. I have had a difficult time accepting the different life path in store for my independent, spiritual self.

Freshman year of college in Colorado, I fell madly, passionately in love with that soprano—willing even to give my life for her. We were both "good" girls: religious people-pleasers, achieving and making everyone proud. We both had boyfriends and we belonged.

Then the shock. I had heard only horrible things about homosexuals, how they were "perverts," bad seeds, people who were nothing like rule-following, religious me. I wanted to be conventional, to fit in, to have the family I had dreamed of my whole life.

Though I didn't judge my natural feelings of love, I suddenly feared a future of firebombs through my windows and a lifetime of harassment if anyone were to know the truth about me.

Younger people today might find this ridiculously over-dramatic. But homosexuality was criminal in many states in 1965, not to mention a target of hatred for some preachers and politicians who were powerful men. I could have been kicked out of college, kicked out of my family, subjected to shock treatments, even institutionalized. My dreams of being in the Peace Corps were crushed, as I knew I could be blackmailed or sent home if anyone discovered my secret.

I was furious to hear people talk of choice and lifestyle. Why would anyone *choose* to be gay in those scary, homophobic days if they could be anything else? I spent the next twelve years trying to find a man I could love as deeply as a woman. On my thirtieth birthday, knowing the risks but needing to live honestly, I finally chose to openly accept my lesbian self. I was certain I would no longer belong.

I didn't want to be part of churches of people saying, "love the sinner, hate the sin." And yet I always remained connected to my own personal God-force, who was not assigned to any race, religion, gender or orientation.

One thread of continuity, from 1963 through 2022, weaves through the faded tan Chapbook beside me now. As a teenager in the mountains near Big Bear, I took this little treasure of worship resources and camp songs for my morning quiet time by the creek bed. Loch Leven Church Camp was a place where I knew I belonged. It offered what I loved most: gathering in nature with a small tribe of people to know one another more authentically, to discuss life, to feel there is a power greater than us, to share our feelings and beliefs in safe circles.

Then, as now, I love being with a small group in natural beauty, asking "what's it all about, Alfie?" Sharing meals, singing together, making crafts or writing, laughing in bunkrooms, awakening to the sounds of birds and breezes in the trees.

Then, as now, I love many of the hymns and songs from this Chapbook, like "Peace, I Ask of Thee, O River," "God, Who Touchest Earth with Beauty," "Dona Nobis Pacem," and "For the Beauty of the Earth." I now change the words to be inclusive, but still feel grounded in the tradition of spiritual seekers who felt such joy in creation that they put poetic words to music.

The songs in this book are also the songs I sang at my childhood summer camping trips, riding along with my parents and brothers in our Nash Rambler station wagon. We pitched our heavy army surplus tent among Redwoods or Giant Sequoias, unloading sleeping bags, blackened pots, and an ax to chop wood and pound tent stakes. I belonged in this singing, God-loving, nature-loving family.

As a single lesbian, I've never had the type of family my parents or friends have. I often feel the pain of being childless. Fortunately, I have found belonging with loving friends who are my family of choice.

I have finally come home to myself and feel a sense of belonging in the Universe. When I write words or music, create photo gifts of nature or inspiration, teach and empower others, or share with friends near and far to honor each other's life path, I feel connected to them all.

What a relief to find my own belonging again after many years of wandering in uncharted territory, wishing for guideposts in the frightening and sometimes exciting unknown. These days, I reclaim my belonging to my whole, ever-healing self.

It is transforming to reframe my story in these greater truths of who I have always been. What a privileged, blessed life I have received along with deep pain. I belong, as do we all, to a grander story. Thank you, God.

***

Dana Curtin has enjoyed many mini careers after training as a French teacher, including brief stints in TV, public relations, and educational test writing in Los Angeles. In the Bay Area, she's had thrilling jobs in training, software, small press publishing, and writing. Now retired, Dana lives in California, the Carolinas, or "around." She believes Guided Autobiography is life changing.

36

The Adoption

by Cathy Lange

A t thirty-one, I was still single. I'd been in two long-term relation-ships, but no offers of marriage until Warren. We'd been dating only two months when he popped the question. I was stunned. We had yet to declare our feelings. I quickly asked myself, *could I live with this man for the rest of my life?* I believed I could, accepted his proposal, and awkwardly said "I love you." Words I felt obliged to say.

Neither of us knew if we wanted children and my career was just beginning to blossom. I was working, attending university part-time, and training to qualify for the Boston Marathon. Yet something felt missing—a baby. A child would give me real purpose, an identity. I'd belong to the club known as "Mothers," and there would be a day every year celebrating my monumental and extraordinary feat.

I imagined the feel of a small, warm hand in mine. A little girl who looked like me, with blonde hair and her father's blue eyes, but she seemed ethereal—a puff of smoke, impossible to grasp. Was this a sign of things to come?

A year later I still wasn't pregnant. Naturally, the "problem" wasn't with Warren: I had blocked fallopian tubes. Like the Berlin Wall, nothing was getting in or out. After announcing to a packed waiting room that I most assuredly had an STD, the doctor handed over a bottle of antibiotics and said my husband should see his doctor. I staggered back to the car. If it wasn't enough to be mocked by a red stain on the toilet paper each month, now I'd been stabbed in the heart with a scarlet letter.

Gratefully, neither my doctor nor husband agreed with the pronouncement of perceived sins. We made an appointment with a fertility specialist—a jocular fellow whose humour did not amuse. He described how he could unfurl the offending tubes as one would unroll a pair of socks. He'd make small incisions in my belly button and above the pubic bone, insert "a knife and fork" and, voilà, unlock the gateway to my ovaries. The specialist also pointed out, however, that in my late 30s, my eggs were exceeding their expiration date. In vitro, he stated, was our best hope.

The nails were closing on the coffin lid of our chances, so I agreed to the operation. I desperately wanted to get pregnant naturally, not with a potential hundred-thousand-dollar debt of IVF.

After the surgery, and with renewed hope, my husband and I attempted coitus every other day during ovulation. I enticed him with lingerie, bubble baths, candles and wine—opportunities I thought most men would jump at.

He didn't.

"It's too much pressure," he said.

As my chances of pregnancy dwindled, so did our relationship.

Menopause ended any small hope I had of getting pregnant and at the same time bolstered my courage to end a difficult marriage after twenty-one years. Then, four years into being single again, I was hit with a proverbial bolt of lightning. There was no reason my dream couldn't still come true. I'd foster a baby!

I dutifully filled out lengthy applications with three agencies, anticipating immediate responses. Days passed, then weeks. Nothing. *Am I too old? Is it because I'm single? Maybe fostering isn't meant for me; I should just plow ahead and adopt.*

Once again, I completed intake applications. By the time I'd reached the end of the second onerous online form, I almost expected to be asked why I failed the recorder in third grade.

"How is it that teenagers and couples get pregnant at the drop of a hat and are never asked how they will raise their baby, discipline their child, or provide access to outdoor spaces to run and play?" I lamented to a friend.

Within days, I received responses to both applications.

"Could you send photos and videos of where you live and include the nearby greenspace you mentioned?"

My sloping shoulders and hunched back quickly straightened. With renewed vigor, I once again believed I could join my four sisters in motherhood.

My hopes were soon dashed. Due to Covid, there was a shortage of adoptees. Most were boys or children with health or behavioural issues that I felt ill equipped to manage.

Then it happened: a little girl located in Mexico. Could I bring her to my forever home? I fell in love with her photos immediately. She was six months old, petite and blonde with brown eyes—like mine. This was the baby I'd waited decades for.

Ten days later, I met her for the first time in a clandestine midnight meeting in a Costco parking lot. *Is this even legal?* When I finally held her in my arms and inhaled the scent of baby sweat, stale airplane air and a distant sunny land, I didn't care. We drove home with her head in my lap, a bonded pair. I changed her name from Dakota to Poppy and took her shopping for pink and turquoise accessories—like the ribbons I wore as a child, tied to the ends of my braids.

When we are out, people pass by us with their babies and we smile, knowingly. They stop and admire my little girl. "How old is she? She's so cute!"

But the greatest compliment came from a friend who said, "She's a skinny mini, just like her mom!"

I'm finally a member of a club, with a little girl who looks just like me. And, if you haven't already guessed... Poppy is a dog.

***

Cathy Lange is a retired executive and unofficial keeper of her family's history. She recently attended a course on memoir writing and guided autobiography and now she's hooked. Cathy lives in New Westminster, British Columbia with her dog and cat. She is writing (haphazardly) her first movie script.

37

She's Got to Be Somebody's Baby

by Amanda J. Smith

I was the youngest of three daughters in a traditional nuclear family. Christian faith was central to our family life. We belonged to a conservative church and my sisters and I attended a small Christian school where our father was the headmaster. Mainstream society, we were taught, was "worldly" and "sinful." We did not have a TV in our home and we listened mostly to Christian or classical music. I didn't consider myself sheltered because I knew no other way of life.

That changed for me when my father's job ended and we had to switch to public school. I skipped fifth grade and entered sixth at the age of ten, a tiny fish in the big pond of a large public junior high school.

Suddenly all the peer pressures of junior high were upon me—and I was not ready. There were so many things I didn't know about, so many cultural references I didn't understand. I quickly realized how sheltered I had been. I wanted desperately to belong among my new classmates, knowing I would have to change myself to fit in. My home-made and hand-me-down clothes were not socially acceptable, so I learned to cobble together outfits that looked somewhat fashionable to avoid being teased. I wasn't allowed to listen to rock stations on the radio at home, but to my great joy the bus driver always had the radio playing. I heard so many popular songs for the first time during those long bus rides. Rod Stewart singing "If you want my body and you think I'm sexy" sounded so scandalous that I couldn't believe it was allowed on the airwaves. But I loved it.

This desire to belong among my mainstream peers would drive my life decisions for many years to come. I tried to keep up with fashion trends, I memorized pop song lyrics, and whenever I went to a friend's house, I would beg to watch their TV. I discarded any notions I had been taught about the sinfulness of the world and embraced the world instead. I just wanted to be and feel like a *normal* kid.

Midway through high school, a new motivation emerged for me—I wanted to experience romance. My head was filled with romantic stories and fantasies from popular love songs and movies. I wanted to belong *to* someone, romantically. Certain song lyrics struck a note with me, like Rick Springfield's "Jessie's Girl" and "Somebody's Baby" by Jackson Browne: "Just look at that girl with the lights coming up in her eyes; She's got to be somebody's baby, she must be somebody's baby." I wanted nothing more than to be somebody's girl. I did have a boyfriend for a brief shining moment in my junior year, but he broke up with me after only two months. I blamed myself for not being "cool" enough.

When I turned eighteen, I moved out of my parents' house to escape the repression of home and experience college life fully as an adult. And I did. I met a boy my first quarter and had a wonderful time exploring adulthood and my newfound freedom. Discarding the constraints of my childhood, I went to frat parties and danced and drank alcohol. After a while, I broke up with my college boyfriend and dated around quite a lot, enjoying every bit of that.

I met my husband junior year of college: my handsome dream man, older and established in a career as a paramedic. We fell in love in a whirlwind, got engaged within a few months, and married within a year. Shortly after, he was hired by a fire department and began his career as a firefighter paramedic. I happily wore a gold neck charm that said "Fireman's Lady." The license plate frame on my car read "I am my Fireman's Flame." That was my identity. I belonged to somebody, and I was deliriously happy about it.

Determined to be a perfect wife, I shaped my identity to be whatever I thought he wanted. For the first fifteen years of marriage, I was content to belong to him and to the "work hard/play hard" social group of his fellow firefighters and their wives. I remained always conscious of the ways I needed to adjust myself to fit in and be liked. But somewhere along the way, the pressures of his job led to escalating alcoholism and the facade of our perfect marriage began to crumble. It took me a few more years to realize the fantasy was over. Just before I began taking steps to leave, he was diagnosed with stage four colon cancer and died within a year—leaving me a widow at the age of forty-one.

A year later, I sold our house and moved to San Diego, California, a city I had always loved but never dreamed I could live in. I bought a perfect-for-me house and have spent ten years building a life that centers on my own desires, dreams and goals. For the first time, I no longer see the need to change myself to fit in. My sense of belonging is solid. After a lifetime of just wanting to belong— among my peers, to my husband—I now belong only to myself. And I will never live any other way.

***

Amanda J. Smith is new to memoir writing and happy to finally be putting her English degree to good use and exploring her childhood dream to be a writer. A former full-time mom and substitute teacher, she now lives in San Diego with her three dogs.

38

The Johor Bahru Happy and Joyous Club

by Lee-Jean Fung

"Why another same morning greeting in our main group? It's jamming up my handphone space!"

"How nice and wonderful to receive so many birthday wishes on my birthday. Thank you, love you."

"Oh no! Our beloved Jennifer passed away last night."

"When is the next outing?"

"Yes, I am bored at home."

"Interesting zoom workshops on the way. And they're free of charge."

This is the Johor Bahru Happy and Joyous Club chat group, formed more than ten years ago. We complain a lot about the non-stop messages clogging our phone space, and yet we've grown to like them. We look at the chat first thing in the morning and its the last thing before we sleep. Why remain in a chat group when we are so frustrated by it at times? Because we feel the empathy of others, especially when the subject is ourselves.

Can you get a sense of belonging from a chat group? Yes!

With my infection of the dreaded coronavirus in early September 2021 and admission to a hospital away from home, I was afraid for my aged parents, who were in another hospital. Messages from the chat group were welcome—soothing to my mind, body and soul to know that there were many others who cared for us and our family members.

"When you are dead, you don't know you are dead. The pain is felt by others. The same thing happens when you are stupid!" This message from last Friday struck me with how true it is, and I was challenged to look beyond my own perspective. At times, I may think that I did the best thing without realising others look at it differently. And so a poem or phrase awakens us, reminds us, motivates us—self-reflection with self-realization occurs. The message is noble, regardless of the messenger. A chat group is full of the same messages we say to each other in person. When we can't see each other, our chat group fills the space where there would otherwise be silence.

One morning, a routine message is noticeably missing from a regular contributor. *What happened?* Calls go unanswered. A group of concerned members go to her house. Her sister says she was hospitalised, but all is well now. To belong is more than your presence being welcome; it's also that your absence is noticed and raises alarm from the other members.

Dozens of "Happy Birthday" greetings to the birthday person. We feel their joy and embrace their happiness. Messages of seasonal, festive greetings. Sometimes repetitious, or in unfamiliar languages. And it's ok. We forgive the space they take up because of the empathy they bring.

"It's almost midnight. I am alone and afraid. I can't sleep. Who can I call to talk to?"
"I am available, you can call me."

There's a first grandchild celebration. "Let's rejoice with Pauline, with Lea Hua." More grandchildren announcements. What glorious moments to rejoice with our friends!

"I am flying over to Australia to see my daughter and her family. What do you all want from Australia?" Wishes flying all over, blessings and joyous messages.

"It's raining heavily at my place, how about yours?" Care and concern for one another.

"Are we going for an outing? When? Is it safe?"

"Yes, the restrictions have been lifted. Let's go in a busload like pre-Covid times. Hooray!"

On a monthly basis, members share their stories online via Zoom. This time our golden girls, Sis Hiang and Sis Yiew, will be sharing their innermost secrets and gems of their lives. Every month, two members share. Another platform for public speaking, fellowship and learning from one another. What a wonderful activity for self-discovery, to unleash our potential and be useful.

"I will be away for two weeks, please take care of my mail in the mailbox and 'patrol' my house if anyone is on the way."

"Will do, no problem."

"Let's meet at our daily zoom for 30 minutes of laughter and uplift our mood for the whole day. Chair Fitness exercise too, twice a month."

"We are having face-to-face activities again, laughter exercises and drum circle sessions at the outdoor open space...Ye-eeah! Every Friday at Taman Pelangi, near Toast Cafe...Yippee!"

Photos and videos of past and present memories flood the chat group. Who cares? We care. We will watch them, then save or delete them—the choice is ours. We can read and watch them over and over with smiles on our faces.

Future plans and exciting news are discussed in the group in real time, giving us something to look forward to.

We belong in this group of people, sharing the common goal of being happy and joyous. The chat group revitalises us and moves us forward. The connection keeps us alive. Like a virtual house that is big enough for us all, where we notice when someone is missing from the table. Together, through messages, photos, and videos, we rejoice, we laugh, we cry, we argue, we love, we empathise, we joke, we smile, we dislike, we like, we sing, and we dance.

That's the Johor Bahru Happy and Joyous Club chat group.

***

Lee-Jean Fung is retired from a thirty-five-year career as a pharmacist. A life-long learner and Laughter Yoga Master Trainer, she is also founder of the Johor Bahru Happy and Joyous Club, a Non-Governmental Organization whose main activities are Laughter Yoga, Clowning, Drum Circle and activities pertaining to happy and joyous lifestyles. Lee-Jean lives in Johor Bahru, Malaysia and her vision is to have Laughter groups in all parks of Johor Bahru.

39

Waffles vs. Eggs

by Lisa Culhane

I don't remember exactly when my stomach began to hurt.

I know it wasn't when we were all piled on my parents' bed, amidst the Sunday funny papers, the dog, and the giggling. And I know it wasn't when my mom suggested we start our day with waffles for breakfast.

But sometime between the breakfast suggestion and the rest of Sunday, the dull ache started—usually well before the yelling and screaming.

No matter what I did, I found myself powerless to stop the outburst, although sometimes it felt like I could forestall it through impeccable behavior. Controlling my behavior was the only superpower I possessed; but unlike invisibility, teleportation, or alchemy, it never proved very useful.

Yet every week, I would give it a try. I would scurry about, helping with chores as best I could. Despite my effort, the explosion would eventually arrive. Someone in the house would invariably trip the invisible wire and KABOOM! My mom would go crazy, personifying the term "ranting and raving."

By evening, the storm would pass, but not the wariness lodged in my stomach. And thus, most Sundays would end with me and the dull ache settling in to watch The Wonderful World of Disney and Wild Kingdom.

As an adult, I knew I wanted Sundays to be both the same and different. I wanted the time in bed with the whole family, the laughter, the reading, and the playing with the dog—followed by a yummy breakfast. I longed for the sense of belonging that clung to those memories of Sunday mornings. I just didn't want the dread and fear that followed.

In the early years of marriage, my husband and I would start Sundays off reading the paper in bed with the dog at our feet, followed by a run and a breakfast of potatoes and eggs, and then a second cup of coffee as we enjoyed more of the Sunday paper. As our family expanded and the paper moved online, we continued with mostly the same tradition. First, the kids would climb into our bed and we would read books together, amongst the dog and the laughter. We'd get up for a run that first involved a stroller and eventually kids on bikes, followed by Sunday breakfast.

It sounds good now, but for years I found myself peeved almost every Sunday morning. It wasn't the heaviness or stomachache of my childhood, but it tempered the mood. The irritation would start as we headed home from our run, when my husband said he would get a breakfast of eggs and potatoes started. Sometimes I suggested we go out or make pancakes or waffles instead, but he would override the suggestion. Even when the rest of us voted for waffles, his vote would win. It sounds like nothing, but it irritated me. And even when I didn't suggest something different, I still felt overridden. Because it seemed so petty, it took me years to mention this.

When I did finally bring it up, something amazing happened. My husband told me that when he was growing up, his family also had many rituals, including one on Sunday mornings. And when his parents got divorced in his early teens, most of these rituals were discarded. Neither of his parents was inclined to continue their family traditions, choosing instead to start fresh. From then on, he craved the sense of connection that ongoing rituals provided. Eating the exact same thing every Sunday morning felt important because it was a routine he could easily maintain.

Truthfully, I had never considered the contents of a weekly meal ritualistic. Sure, I loved serving my Nana's special dressing on Thanksgiving and always made cinnamon rolls on Christmas morning. But in childhood, when my family gathered at Nana's every Friday night, what we ate wasn't the point. And the weekly potato breakfast? I just hadn't thought of it that way. But when he shared why he wanted potatoes and eggs every Sunday, my ire disappeared. Suddenly, it felt like an honor to share that same breakfast each week.

Now our kids are grown and flown. They still come home for vacations and weekends here and there, but their day-to-day lives play out a thousand miles away. When they do come home, they always try to schedule their departure sometime after potatoes and eggs. It's a ritual they have come to count on and love.

As for me, I appreciate how our family's Sunday morning ritual evolved when we melded the good parts from our childhood memories. By combining the pieces we loved into something meaningful, we were able to rewrite negative parts of our childhood scripts and create something we both cherish.

The Waffles vs. Eggs debate helped me to see that I actually had another superpower after all. Alchemy is the practice of changing something ordinary into something extraordinary. It is that bit of magic that transformed something as ordinary as a potato and egg breakfast into a ritual that creates a deep sense of rootedness and belonging.

***

Lisa Culhane believes our stories are deeply personal, but their essence is almost always universal. Passionate about helping people find, write, and share their unique stories, she is a life and writing coach who lives in Denver, Colorado with her husband, dog, and wanderlust.

40

Outside the Frame

by Evelyn Levine

H is shocking reaction brought the fractious argument to a dead stop. He had thrown the tree down the stairs. There it lay, smushed between the dryer and the wall, its paper chains dangling pathetically. Both children were wailing and my tears were close. After a moment of staring at each other in stunned silence, he made a quick exit, followed by the predictable house-shaking door slam. And that was it for holiday trees in our family.

The year was 1980, the children ages seven and four. Unlike my protected ghetto-like childhood, theirs was taking place in a non-Jewish environment. Paul was the sole Jewish child in his elementary school, and Rachel the only one in her daycare. When the daycare held a small Christmas parade, each preschooler carried a homemade stocking made of green and red felt. But our girl, the smallest of the group, led the little procession bearing her blue felt Hanukkah dreidel. It was a well-meant gesture by the daycare teachers; but like many such attempts, it served to highlight separation rather than inclusion.

That daycare parade touched a deep chord buried in my own childhood memories of 1950s Montreal. As a little girl, I may have been mostly sheltered in my homogeneous Jewish neighbourhood. But I still felt a bit outside of the frame, especially around Christmas. At eight years old, I made my own Christmas stocking. The next morning, my mother spotted it carefully taped to my bedroom wall. "Now what the Sam Hill...?" One of Mother's 1940s expressions to convey surprised disapproval. She was staring at a stretched out, child-sized athletic sock hanging precariously by Scotch tape.

"Evie, come here." She was kneeling on the rug. "What is this?"

"It's nothing," I mumbled as my cheeks reddened. "It's just a game."

"A game? What kind of game? And you shouldn't make a mess with tape on the walls. What is it anyway?" I knelt down and gently removed it, cradling it in my lap.

"A Christmas stocking," I whispered.

"A what?"

"A Christmas stocking I made."

"I see. You made a stocking. What's in it?"

"Stuff."

"Show me."

I poked my hand inside and began removing objects one by one: a doll's dress, a miniature sombrero, a green lollipop (slightly sticky), and my treasured miniature beer stein with its fancy flip-up lid. She surveyed the items and looked at me, her face softening.

"So, are these gifts to yourself?" she asked, incredulous.

"Unh hunh," I nodded, tears brimming.

She put her arm around me.

"What made you do that, sweetheart?"

"I dunno, I can't explain...maybe I wish we did Christmas. All the TV shows have everyone doing Christmas. My favourite part is the stockings. They put little, tiny toys in stockings and I love little, tiny toys. Why can't we do that?"

"We don't do that because it's not our holiday, not our tradition."

I sighed, a tear rolling down my cheek. Mummy wiped it with her ever-present hankie and stroked my head.

Twenty-five years later, the tree episode had grown out of that memory fragment. I was trying to make the December holiday dilemma easier for my children. They were inundated by Christmas rituals. At Paul's school, every December morning began with a piano rolled out into the central corridor. The entire school gathered around to sing carols. Every classroom had a decorated tree, and the children drew lots for gift buddies. My children felt outside the frame, just as I had.

I devised a strategy. I would buy a live Norwegian Island pine tree in a planter. It was perfect, I reasoned, as it was Christmas tree-ish, but not a true Christmas tree. Afterwards, it could just be a house-plant. We'd decorate it with stars of David and blue and white paper chains. It would be our Hanukkah bush. Not a wholly original idea, but certainly new to my family. The children and I had a delight-ful time cutting, gluing, and draping chains around the tree's sparse branches. They made their best efforts at fashioning the stars, pasting misshapen triangles atop each other. We sang Hanukkah songs mixed with "Rudolph the Red-Nosed Reindeer." It was a sweet time.

We were just standing back to admire our work when Joe came home.

"What's this?" he said, displeasure evident on his face. The children chorused, "It's our Hanukkah bush, Daddy. Isn't it pretty?"

"No!" he spluttered, staring directly at me. "That's a Christmas tree. We don't have Christmas trees in this house!" This prompted a clamour of responses.

"But Daddy, it's not a Christmas tree. Can't you see the blue and white chains and our stars of David?"

And from me with quavering voice, "Joe, be reasonable. It's a way for them to feel more comfortable at this fraught time of year. A way for them to belong. Think about it. It's different for them than it was for us as kids."

"Bullshit, that's just bullshit!" he bellowed. And that's when he grabbed the tree by its spindly top branch and half-threw, half-pushed it down the eight stairs to the laundry room.

Fast forward forty-one years to December 2021. I sip eggnog as I help decorate the Christmas tree in my daughter's living room. My son-in-law has just affixed the shimmering silver star to the top. A wireless speaker plays a mix of carols and Hanukkah songs. We're a bit short on baubles. Granddaughter has an idea. "How about we use the shiny Hanukkah banner Grandma brought us?" So we drape the golden "Happy Hanukkah" letters across the branches.

As we work, I can't help remembering that smashed tree of long ago. I realize that somehow, I found a way for my kids to be comfortably Jewish in a non-Jewish world. They definitely don't live outside the frame.

*****

Evelyn Levine is a retired speech-language pathologist and part-time writer. She has taken Guided Autobiography courses as well as a recent Writers' Room. She has lived in four Canadian cities. Four years ago, she reunited with the love of her youth and lives happily with him amid the many trees of Vancouver, Canada.

We Cheer for the Indians

by Don Donato

The flexible, red salt-cedar switch wraps a stinging slap around my face, leaving a small slit over my left eyebrow and a burning welt across my right cheek.

"Talk American, goddammit!" snarls the blocky teacher with the constant growl on her face, as she lays the switch across the forehead of the boy I'd spoken with in Navajo. My acquaintance got it worse, wearing a line of blood dripping across his forehead and down his jawline.

The six-foot switches give teachers on duty quite the reach as they catch the elementary school kids speaking softly to each other in Navajo or Apache while in line for the "coloreds" biffys—far from the school office and smelling like a campground outhouse. Brutally cold in winter and claustrophobically hot in spring and fall.

Eyes full of fury, the Navajo holds his tongue. Speaking out gets more lashes you must later explain to a parent who insists you must have done more than speak Navajo to get such welts. "No, Mom, honest. That's really all it takes!" She doesn't believe me. It's been a rough start in Winslow, Arizona.

Back inside, my desk is easy to find—center of a row that I share with no one. Nothing but empty desks in front of and behind me.

My California milieu consisted of Japanese, French, Irish, Swedish, English, Dutch, Germans, Scotts, and Italians. Methodists, Baptists,

Catholics, agnostics, Jews and Shintos who got along and watched out for each other. So, I don't understand racism.

I ask my teacher. "You're our only half-breed," she says gently. "You are dark. Your Indian daddy is darker, but your momma is very light-skinned. So, that's why you have your own row. Honestly, we weren't sure how the Negro or Indian children might react if we put you in one of their rows."

So, *special,* but not like, "Welcome!"

More aware, I notice now how I have to buy my pop from a side window (warm instead of cold), while white kids sit at tables inside, enjoying their malts and shakes. At movie theaters, those of us without white skin sit in the balcony, out of sight. But we cheer loudly for the "Indians" whenever it's a western.

In 1954, this is still very much The West, where a person is judged on two things: how dark their skin is and whether they can draw. Nearly every boy and girl has a cap pistol holster rig. The theater offers a free Saturday movie ticket to any kid who can fast-draw a pistol and beat the timing device. I got a two-gun cap pistol rig for Christmas two years ago, but it is so clearly a toy that I'm embarrassed to bring it.

I'm in line on the colored side at the theater when my high-school neighbor, Steve, beats the timer. He invites me to sit with him and his friends, but the usher stops us at the door. "He goes to the balcony," she says in a satisfied tone. Steve is frozen to the spot, dumbfounded. When the shock passes, he gives a kind of half-salute, "See you back home, kid."

That afternoon Steve is at my house, asking my mom if he can borrow me for a while. We head out to the Carson family's garage.

"Know anything about guns?" he asks. I answer in the affirmative, and he points to the two-gun rig sitting on the workbench. "Show me."

Compared to my cheesy toy pistols, these are gorgeous: thirty-two caliber Colts snug in their well-oiled holsters. I reach over and grab hold of one and look at Steve. He nods. Carefully, I check the chamber of each pistol to make sure they are empty and return them to their holsters.

Steve says, "Pretty good. So these are unloaded now, eh?" Another test, which I recognize, and so I smile and answer, "treat every gun as if it's always loaded."

Then I notice Steve's mom standing in the door of the garage, watching. She smiles at me. "Steve told me what happened at the movie theater. We don't approve. I want to loan you my fast draw rig so that you can get in for free from now until kingdom come."

As she turns to go back in the house, Steve tells me that their family hobby is fast-draw competitions, and his mother is number two in Arizona. He looks pretty proud.

We walk two blocks to the edge of the desert. Using a small hill as a backstop, I practice drawing and firing. Day after day.

Saturday comes, and I join the parade of holstered kids en route to the theater. "Jesus!" blurts a florid-faced man in a cowboy shirt and a Stetson, "There's a Injun here with a real two-gun rig!"

"Hell, boy, them's not cap guns, are they? Di'ja steal 'em?"

"No," I say, indignant. "My neighbor let me borrow them for the fast-draw."

As other kids step up and fail to beat the clock at one second or less, the men mutter to each other, flipping through the rule sheets.

Finally, after a careful examination, the men give the pistols back. "Aw, shit, Earl. Them's heavier than cap guns, and now we know he ain't got no live ammo, let him try. They's no way he can beat the clock."

It's the exact same model as the clock I've practiced with. My right forefinger lightly holds down the start button, and when I let up—lightning! The right pistol fires but the clock needle doesn't move. The flustered men mutter, "now the damn clock's busted," and decide I should try the left-hand pistol. Same result. "Yep," they agree, "busted timer."

The men wave me off to the side, moving the line along. Next kid tries—the "pop" sound stops the clock at two seconds. It's not broken. "Hell, I'll get my rig," grumbles a stringbean of a man. "If the kid beats me, he gets in free every Saturday for a year." Stringbean stalks off to a nearby pickup truck.

And that's how I spent each Saturday for a year in the balcony, remembering the sight of those red blank-paper wads bouncing off the chest of the cowboy whose Colt had yet to clear leather. All three times, frustrating the men who insist on trying again in case it's some fluke.

Among the "colored" kids, my legend begins.

***

Don Donato is a retired newspaperman and pastor. He holds a B.S. from CU/Pueblo and an M.Div. from Iliff School of Theology, Denver. Inspired by Ernest Hemingway's advice to "only write what you know," Don has enriched his knowledge base by running the gamut from babysitting for large families, to cleaning septic tanks. He retired in Willmar, Minnesota, with his gracious third and final wife.

42

˙Underfoot

by Ada Gates

I got my first pony at four years old and never looked back. Every waking moment that I was not in school, I could be found in the barn or tearing through the woods on a long succession of ponies and horses. Our big house on Long Island was a paradise of woods, gardens, and lawns—an entire world for us all. In a childhood as idyllic as mine—gloriously wrapped up in a big, loving, boisterous, crazy family with seven vibrant siblings—every day was an adventure, full of excitement.

Every night, my mother tucked each of us into bed with a kiss goodnight, murmuring "sweet dreams." We went to sleep happy, loved, safe, and protected. The next day always shimmered with expectation in my mind.

Our home was a place of nonstop discovery, redolent with books, paintings, and music. Opening a book on Africa, the Rockies, or Europe, I was instantly enthralled. I wanted to go to those places and drink them all in. My beneficent parents understood that children self-select and let us all choose our passions and our destinies.

As a young adult living in New York City, I sought out work that I loved, a new place where I could bloom. I loved dance and theater. It was a heady city, New York, and I wanted to explore it to the full.

I dove in with both feet and swirled through off-Broadway theater and out-of-town repertory, dancing six hours a day in modern studios.

No instant success, of course. As other work evolved, I wanted five or six lives so I could live each and every one for years.

I became a jack of all trades, master of none. And I felt ashamed that I was never really good at any one thing. Watching others succeed, I fell short. Looks and spirit couldn't replace hard work and talent. I wanted celebrity without surrendering to the craft. Years followed of fearful wondering. *Who was I? What would I do?*

Prayers are answered even when you don't know you're praying. On a lark of a car trip out West, I found myself in the Rockies of Colorado. While knocking around as a waitress, I got a horse but couldn't find a horseshoer. I certainly had time to go to horseshoeing school, so I did. Me and forty-nine guys. At twenty-seven, I was older than everybody else. What a travail, but I stuck it out.

What started as "I'll shoe my own horse" turned into people calling for my services. *Wow*—shocked, surprised—*wow, this is great. I love this. I'm with horses, I'm outside, I'm meeting new people, and making a living for the first time ever.* I surrendered to doing this one thing that just got better and better. I wanted to do it more and more.

The first half of my life was like tumbling around in a dryer; the second half began when I found work I truly loved. I left jack of all trades to become master of one. It was still turbulent, but with direction and drive. My brother called me unstoppable. I never noticed that I didn't "belong" in a man's job. It felt normal to me. Life had come full circle. The years of dance had given me legs for shoeing, the years of riding ponies had given me horses all the time. I could finally make a living doing what I loved.

I remember coming home to my little Colorado house at the end of a long day dragged around corrals shoeing ranch horses. People paid me in cash. I'd sit on my bed and lay out all the money, neatly stacking the fives, tens and twenties in piles. *Look at all this. I made this. Somebody paid me for this work.* It felt wonderful. It felt new and solid and good. It was the happiest time of my life. All alone, but happy, excited, drinking in each day. I plunged deeply, committed like I had never been before.

As I progressed to the big-time (racetracks in California), fear bubbled under the surface. *Am I good enough?* Up 'til then, nobody would train me. But I kept showing up and learning anyway. Whether overcoming fear or overcoming challenges, the walls got lower and the leaps got higher. Not effortless, but full of joy.

I found myself.

During forty years as a horseshoer, I attained heights I never could have imagined. It was real. I was of service, helping horses, making a living, as fit and strong as a dancer.

At Santa Anita Racetrack in 1977, I asked yet another man, "Would you help me learn more?" He shot back, "Sure." A man without judgment or criticism, he accepted me, trained me, became my mentor, became really my all. He was a divine man; I was so lucky he actually loved me. We married and I felt the unconditional love I had felt long ago in my family. I felt I had it all, and I did.

I went from being given a life where I belonged to making a life where I belonged. A blessed life.

***

Ada Gates was the first woman licensed to shoe thoroughbred racehorses in the US and Canada. She has written numerous farrier articles, appeared on David Letterman, and is a member of the American Farrier's Hall of Fame. Raised in Long Island, New York, Ada now studies writing in a community of three hundred PhD earners in Pomona, California.

43

Not Just an Old Photograph

by Val Perry

This is the story of how my great-grandmother's photograph helped me find belonging in America.

When I married my American G.I. husband in my home country of England and flew overseas to a new life, I could not imagine how lost I would feel without everything familiar and dear to me. It was 1972, and I had never been away from my family for any length of time. My first home stateside was Rapid City, South Dakota; but as any military spouse knows, the career comes with multiple moves. The following year we were reassigned to Massachusetts, just outside Boston.

With the birth of my only child, a special needs baby, the loss of family and friends was further amplified. Oh! How I wished I could call my mother on those long nights when I had no clue why our baby girl would not stop crying. But overseas calls were expensive back then. Imagine my excitement when my parents and brother flew over from England to visit us in 1976.

Dad came through the gates at Logan Airport carrying two gifts—one from each of my grandmothers. My mother's mother, Nan Miller, sent a large chiming clock I had always admired when it sat on her mantlepiece. The second gift was a sepia-toned, postcard-sized photograph protected inside a brown cardboard cover. Dad found it amongst Grandmother Florence's belongings after she passed and thought I should have it. As he talked, he pointed to something on the cover.

I admit, I did not pay enough attention to the photograph initially. With the excitement of my family's visit, adjusting to motherhood, and getting reassigned to Florida, it was some time before I sat down to look at the photograph again. Inside the worn cover was an image of an older, petite woman sitting at a table. Her hair was neatly braided in a bun and she wore a long, layered, silky dress and shawl in the style of the 1900s. Handwritten across the lower right corner of the photo were the words: To Florence, with love, from Mother.

Since Florence was my grandmother's first name, I assumed the dedication was from my great-grandmother, whose name I did not know. Remembering my father's gesture, I looked where he had pointed. Imprinted on the cover was an address to a photographer's studio located on Beacon Hill, in Boston.

Wait a minute! How did my great-grandmother have her photograph taken in Boston?

For many generations, my family had lived and worked in the East End of London. We were not known as travelers. My father had brought me a mystery, and it remained so for thirty years.

As time passed, I became more determined to find the history behind my great-grandmother's photograph. Sadly, my father had died not long after his visit to America. No one else in the family seemed able to shed light on the photo—no one, that is, until I heard from my cousin Susan. Our fathers were brothers, but we hadn't been in direct contact for forty years when she began genealogical research into our family. Mum told Susan that I had a photo of our great-grandmother. I sent her a photocopy, also mentioning the mysterious Boston connection.

Susan, as it turned out, was like a "dog with a bone" when it came to solving family mysteries. She discovered that our great-grandmother's full name was Mary Ann Smith and she had eight children: four from marriage and four from a later relationship. Two of her grown sons emigrated to Boston, eventually forming a construction company together.

We still did not know how or why Mary Ann came to Boston until Susan found a London newspaper article recounting a terrible accident that resulted in the death of one of Mary Ann's other sons. Shortly after this tragedy, Mary Ann and her only single daughter booked passage on a ship to North America.

Susan then focused her research on Boston and located descendants of one of the sons who had settled in the area. I have my cousin to thank for arranging an incredible meeting with two elderly great-aunts still living in New Bedford, Massachusetts.

In early October 2010, Susan and I flew from England and Florida to meet in Boston. When we arrived at the modest home of Great-Aunt Ella, I truly could not believe, after all these years, that I had genuine relatives living so close to where I had once lived in the Boston suburbs. However, my uncertainty evaporated in an instant when I passed an eighteen-inch antique oval frame hanging at the entrance to Ella's living room. Behind the domed glass was a large copy of the same photograph my father had bequeathed to me all those years earlier.

It is hard to describe the warm feeling I had as I looked upon the familiar image. I no longer felt like an orphan in America.

We spent several wonderful days together with our great-aunts, Ella and May. Susan and I were fussed over by them and treated to a warm welcome by the family. Both great-aunts recalled being children when Mary Ann and her daughter arrived from England to join their household. We learned that Mary Ann's daughter stayed in Boston and married; but after several years, Mary Ann became ill and returned to London.

May and Ella raised ten children between them. I thought about my struggle with new motherhood when I first received Mary Ann's photo. It was as though my great-grandmother was reaching out to me across time, saying, "there is help nearby, find your aunts." Though our meeting came late, I am so happy we finally reconnected.

***

Val Perry was born and raised in London. As an adult, she lived in both the U.S. and England before retiring to Valrico, Florida, with her husband, daughter and tuxedo cat, Gracie. Val has led a life writing program and taught Guided Autobiography classes at her local library for fifteen years.

Garlic and Oranges

by Nandini Bandyopadhyay

W e were on our way to a birthday party, and I was so excited. My ten-month-old child, Spandan, looked so grown up in a new sailor's suit. It had been a little over a month since we came to the USA from India, and this was the first party we were invited to.

Before stepping out of the car, I checked my saree one more time, made sure my baby's shiny shoes were still in place and picked up the gift. As Subrata, my husband, unbuckled Spandan's car seat, I suddenly realized something. Almost all the other guests strolling past us had huge, elaborate bags or boxes wrapped in shiny paper embellished with glitter and bows. I was holding a plastic bag from Walmart with our gift inside. I looked around hoping to find another gift in a nondescript plastic bag like mine, but couldn't. Part of me just died at that moment. Shame and humiliation clouded my eyes. I gripped the handle, not wanting to go in anymore.

Subrata, a little clueless with regard to social cues, wasn't sure what was happening as I refused to leave the car. When he finally ducked inside to ask what was keeping me, I mumbled about the gift and showed him the gray plastic bag.

The gift had exceeded our budget. Subrata was a graduate student and though he had a scholarship, we were on an extremely tight budget. I had spent a lot of time debating about the gift, finally choosing a dress of yellow tulips on an ivory base with scalloped edges, even though it meant cutting corners that month to make up for the extra spending.

Thirty years ago, the concept of gift bags and wrapping paper was not prevalent in India. I had never seen them before, didn't know such a thing existed. In that fleeting moment, I seriously doubted I would ever fit in a country so different from the one I left behind. Tears threatened to spill out, but Subrata was very calm. He put the baby in my lap and nonchalantly took the gift from my hands. He looked at me and started walking into the party and I followed him sheepishly.

But the shame remained. It reminded me that I was so different from the people around me. Then I slowly started to think more rationally. It was not as if I had always fit in.

When I was growing up, Baba (my Dad) moved around for his job. Ma and I tagged along. I always felt a little awkward initially, but then I would adjust—but it was not easy when I became a teenager. The stakes were high, the place was unfamiliar, and people always reminded me that I was an outsider. Middle and high school girls would form cliques and completely ignore me—even if I stood right in front of them. I was the last one picked for activities, even those I was good at. I built a wall around me and spent time reading, painting, or just daydreaming. I realized it was okay to not belong and started taking small pleasure in being different from the crowd.

My college days were another story. Surprisingly, I blended right in. I was social, friendly, and not as shy as before. So, I forgot how it felt to be an outsider. After the move to America, the long last name, the brown skin in a small, predominantly Caucasian southern town, the requests to repeat my accented words over and over, I again felt small and insignificant. When Spandan went to kindergarten, he was the only non-Christian brown kid in the entire school. He was oblivious to it, but I struggled.

We later moved to Tampa, where I did fit in. It took time, but I felt more comfortable in my skin. I still had the long last name, accent, and brown skin darkened by the sun, but I had stopped worrying about fitting in.

There are still plenty of faux pas, and popular tv shows or movies I have never heard of, but I continue to learn and revise my ways. I adapt at my pleasure, without the pressure of needing to belong.

And then last week, my youngest son Shaurya looked at me and said he's not sure about where he belongs? And I was so taken aback. At twenty-six years old, he is the most well-adjusted person in our family, the one who fits in everywhere. He knows social etiquette, pop culture trivia, and dating rules we never taught him. In fact, when we are in doubt, we always ask him.

Shaurya slowly explained that when he is filling out forms, he selects "Asian" in the race column, but when people look at him, they see a brown man with big, dark eyes. "And I sure don't identify myself as being Indian," he said, "because I have only visited the country a few times and don't feel the same connection that I feel here. I identify myself as an American with Indian origin. But then, why do I feel that people think otherwise?"

So the quest continues for all of us, immigrants or otherwise: the awkward ones who instinctively know that they are different, and the confident ones who seem to know how to fit in. The search for belonging, a place of our own, and a home where we are always welcome.

I recall a picture I saw once of a head of garlic with one orange section snugly fitting into the space of a missing clove. The caption read: Not every place you fit in is where you belong.

***

Nandini Bandyopadhyay is originally from India and has been a resident of the Tampa Bay area since 1998. A former community columnist and book reviewer for The Tampa Tribune, she now works with a not-for-profit organization that raises awareness, educates, and provides mental health support in the South Asian community. Nandini is a published author in her mother tongue.

45

Happy New Year to You!

by Yingchao Xiao

"Y**ou moved again?"** my mother asked on the other end of the line.

"Yes, Mom. And you know what, I bought a house this time."

"A house in California?"

"Yes, and you would like it. It has upturned eave corners, like the Drum Tower in Xi'an." I knew that would please my mother.

"So you didn't forget where you are from," she said.

"Never, Mom."

After shifting from place to place on different continents, at forty-eight I bought my first home in the small foothill town of Sierra Madre, Spanish for "Mountain Mother." From my backyard, I could see the ridges of the San Gabriel Mountains during the day and the moon, round or sickle, in the dark blue sky at night. Everything was perfect, except the demographic data.

Among the 10,578 Sierra Madre residents, less than two percent were Asian—the lowest Asian population in the San Gabriel Valley. My move to Sierra Madre made the Chinese population climb to one percent. For every hundred people, ninety-nine of them looked different from me. I felt like a guest who knocked at a door, was let in, and then stood waiting to be accepted. I decided to work towards that final feeling of acceptance.

I worked late into the evening six days a week, and paid my taxes on time each year. While I could not change the shape of my eyes or the color of my skin, I tried to blend in. I checked out the kinds of books they read from the public library and tried to erase the Chinese accent from my speech. I smiled at everyone I met on the street and admired their gods. However, I still liked to wear my close-fitting Chinese dress and grow organic bok choy in a corner of my backyard. I liked being a "Chinese-American."

Sierra Madre is a town that keeps people, and keeps them for a long time. It kept me. Talking to friends, I began calling it "my town" and the neighborhood "my people." After twenty years of living here peacefully, I finally felt like a small goldfish swimming in a nice pond.

Like they say, it never rains—it pours. When the world was hit by the pandemic in 2020, there was a voice shouting "China Virus" on TV, followed by news that Asians, especially aged Asians, had become a target for hate crimes. Colleagues sent boxes of chocolate to my door and phone calls from friends—Asian, white, black and Latino—came pouring in. Soon, social media sites began releasing videos of Asians being assaulted in New York City, San Francisco, and downtown Los Angeles. Winter holidays passed without celebrations, while theaters and restaurants closed with Covid-19 notices on their front doors. When Chinese New Year was approaching, we were not even prepared to make the traditional dumplings.

On New Year's Eve, I decided to keep my routine—my daily evening walk. Instead of taking my usual route on dark, small streets, I went to the streetlight-lined Sierra Madre Boulevard. In the deep pocket of my jacket I gripped a bottle of pepper spray, thumb on the switch, ready to spray the blinding liquid within two seconds should I be in peril.

Walking on the empty street, I saw my shadow grow long and then short as I passed by each streetlight. Palm trees standing tall on the sidewalks shook their sparse, long leaves, ready to knock me down from behind and bury me somewhere with all my American dreams.

I passed the fire station where volunteer firefighters were on their night shift. I passed Tacos Ensenada where decent fish tacos sold for

$0.99 a piece. I passed the Thai restaurant where the owner once cooked a special fish-soup for me.

Then I saw the neon lights of the Sierra Madre Playhouse, an iconic building in our city. On the left side of its marquee, I read "Happy Lunar New Year" in English, and on the right side the same greeting in pinyin Chinese. I stopped in front of the playhouse, read the greetings once, twice, and three times. I felt something warm come up from my stomach to my throat, nose and eyes. Tears dripped down into my facemask. I began sobbing.

"Are you alright?" An aged couple came from behind with a small dog dressed in a red vest.

I turned to them and pointed to the marquee, exclaiming, "They are greetings to our Lunar New Year!" The couple read the marquee, looked at each other, and shrugged.

"Happy New Year!" I shouted to them, hands waving. The gray-headed woman pulled the leash and they walked away quickly.

"Happy New Year to you too!" I shouted to Sierra Madre Playhouse.

It was unreasonable to expect the old couple to understand my crying in front of the marquee. It was unreasonable to expect anyone on the street to understand the warm lump coming up in my throat. But there were people, like those working in the Sierra Madre Playhouse, who did understand me and my feelings. I was a guest accepted here, and for that, I cried.

***

Yingchao Xiao was born in China and had gone through a turbulent time in her youth. She was a farmer, an electrician, a translator, and then an attorney practicing law in southern California. She's now settled in Sierra Madre, California with her cat Tofu.

46

Barrenness: The Gift That Keeps on Giving

by Sylvia Totzke

D o you remember the Kissing Song? A girl and a boy, sittin' in a tree, K-I-S-S-I-N-G. First comes love, then comes marriage, then comes a baby sitting in a carriage.

The kissing song promised that I would add Betrothed, Wife and Mother to my identity as a woman.

Shortly after our wedding, my mother informed me that she was too young to be a grandmother, so we'd better not even think about having children for a while. We were definitely fine with putting off the "baby sitting in the carriage" part for a while.

A few years later, we felt ready to be parents but our efforts didn't produce a baby sitting in a carriage. We needed professional help, so I made an appointment with a fertility specialist. We did the usual sperm and hormone testing, concluding with my laparoscopy. I was still in the stirrups at my post-surgical appointment when the specialist said that my career goal of dentistry was a great choice for a woman. I was astonished by his comment. Was he telling me there would be no babies? Then he spelled it out for me: my husband's lazy sperm, and low sperm count, coupled with my low hormone levels would make it very difficult to conceive without the help of fertility drugs. If I wanted to, I could start taking them right away.

I left the office dazed and discouraged. I'd seen the emotional toll fertility therapy had taken on others, and I didn't want that for myself. That evening, we discussed the results and decided we didn't want to jump on the roller coaster of fertility therapy. We'd gone as far as we could handle.

"You can always adopt," people said. (Really? If only I had a dime for every time I heard that statement.) We tried to adopt a child. Without prompting or knowing our situation, a well-meaning doctor from our church told us they had a maternity patient. Since the father wasn't interested in raising the child, she planned to place her child for adoption. The doctor thought we would make good parents, so he offered to help us adopt this young woman's baby. Since she was halfway through her pregnancy, we had time to think, save money, prepare and pray that the child would be raised by a mother and a father.

God did answer our prayer, but the baby didn't end up in a carriage at our house. The couple decided to marry and raise their son together. I was happy for them, and sad for us. At that moment, I knew I would not add "Mother" to my identity. Instead, I would add "Barren Woman."

When my mother finally declared that she was old enough to be a grandmother, and that we could have a baby anytime now, I told her that adding "Grandmother" to her identity wasn't going to happen either.

She shrugged her shoulders and simply said it was okay that we weren't able to have children. Over the years, she would laugh and say, "I have perfect grandchildren. They are always so polite and respectful. They never ask for anything."

Once, I told her I wanted to buy an evening gown for our upcoming cruise, but I also needed to buy tires for the car. I was deliberating as to whether I should buy the dress. She stopped me mid-sentence and asked, "Which one of my grandchildren will not have shoes because you bought that dress?" She always had a way of bringing me back to reality and make it sound right.

I did buy the tires, *and* the dress. On our cruise I wore that midnight-blue, sequined Lily Rubin gown twice. I felt and looked fabulous in that dress.

Now, I'm not going to tell you that living a barren life has been easy. Too many times, I've felt the pain of that decision when I least expected it—watching a friend's daughter walk down the aisle on her proud father's arm while her mother beamed with joy, or observing a grandmother and granddaughter enjoying a shared experience at the ballet. At those times, I've felt lonely and knew that I missed out on times of great joy. I also knew that I missed out on times of great sorrow. You can't have one without the other.

My husband and I often joke that we have lots of young friends. We don't have to pay for their college education or their weddings, but they actually listen to our advice because we aren't their parents.

People facing fertility or adoption challenges sometimes ask what it's like not to have children. My heart goes out to them as I listen to their stories. When appropriate, I'll share some of my story and encourage them to keep seeking their own path. And then I pray—for them and for me.

I am grateful that I did the K-I-S-S-I-N-G part so long ago. I'm thankful for where it's taken me, even with the unexpected outcome. I don't wear my identity as a barren woman as a badge of honor or one of shame. It's just who I am, and I am grateful that I have a story to tell.

***

Sylvia Totzke is a retired administrator living with her husband of nearly fifty years in Portland, Oregon. She works on international projects and enjoys dragon boat paddling and spending time with her younger friends.

47

Through Vulnerability

by Galen Tinder

T he five of us—four grad students and one professor—gathered for our last class of the semester in a small, windowless room dominated by an expanse of blackboard in the front. Officially, the course was in group dynamics. Unofficially, it was about whether our inter-relational skills stood us in good stead for a career in the ministry.

On this last day, our teacher (a psychologist and gifted therapist) used the blackboard to leave each student with an image of how he saw us. I was the last up. After looking at me, he drew a large chalk circle. Then, after a pause, he made an emphatic dot six inches outside the circumference. He looked at me again and explained, "This circle is the world. This dot is you." Seeing my puzzled look, he continued, "When the circle reconfigures itself so that it encompasses the dot within it, the dot (that's you!) moves to place itself once more on the outside."

I left class mystified. Over lunch, a classmate clarified, "He is saying you are an outsider." Another classmate added, "And that's the way you like it."

They seemed to agree with our professor, but I didn't get it. I was no loner. I always joined things—sports teams, student associations, committees, student newspapers, civic organizations, political and advocacy groups. I liked being part of things. I pulled my weight, even taking leadership roles. In the dedication page of one of his books, my father had written, *To Galen: Son and Independent Thinker.* I resonated with this. I was always thinking—more independently and better than anybody else in the room, so I thought.

It took me a couple of decades to understand what my professor had been getting at, that there was a difference between being part of the circle, and belonging inside of it.

Despite being a "dot outside the circle," I graduated with a Master of Divinity and tumbled into ministry, pastoring a Lutheran congregation in exurbia New Jersey for ten years. The congregation's budget, membership, and Sunday attendance grew steadily, and I enjoyed the work.

But it did not end well for anyone, as my drinking got increasingly out of hand. By my ninth year, I was concerned less with my parishioners and more with my next drink—where to buy the vodka, how to hide it, and where to get rid of empty airline nips and pint bottles.

During the last several months as pastor, I drank my way through the better part of a pint on Sunday mornings, supplementing clear vodka with frantic raids on thick communion wine (Manischewitz Red, a god-awful concoction) five minutes before the eight thirty and eleven o'clock services. Infused with a vague sense of impunity, I don't remember what I was thinking—likely because I wasn't anymore.

Finally, around 11 p.m. one Saturday night, I was staring at a blank piece of paper in my typewriter where a sermon should have been. Some Saturday nights, a few swigs of vodka could stoke my creative juices. Not this time.

On impulse, I picked up the phone and called my Bishop. In less than forty-eight hours, I was bundled off to a month-long rehab program in nearby Summit.

My fellow drunks—who welcomed me and listened to my requisite self-introduction—were impressed by my background and congratulated me for having already nailed down the spiritual angle of recovery. I was not sufficiently self-aware to disabuse them of this fantasy. In truth, having drunk myself not only out of my congregation but out of the ministry, I didn't have a spiritual thought for the next twenty years.

After thirty-five days, I graduated from rehab into Alcoholics Anonymous. I took well to AA. After a three-day relapse five years in, I found my footing and have now been sober for quite a few years. Recovery was not as simple as not drinking. As a friend eventually told me, I was still hobbled by excessive analyticity. Without realizing it, I was filled with shame. I felt awfully sorry for myself—particularly when my first job out of rehab (selling cars, at which I did not excel) didn't go well.

Our society, dominated by the pell-mell pace and performative superficiality of social media, celebrates instant personality transformations. I am sure it happens this way for some people, but my own slow evolution would not make for a scintillating movie script. People in AA heal through telling their stories and listening to the stories of others. These accounts are not of triumph and conquest, but of failures and defeats, the dead ends that our best thinking and most intense efforts crashed into. Out of these tales arises a community of vulnerability. In this collection of fractured souls, I gradually absorbed the difference between fitting in, being a part of, and true belonging.

My grad school professor did not place me outside the circle of humanity because I thought so well, but because I thought so *much*. My analytic disposition shielded me from emotions—both mine and others'. I had moral principles and could depict empathy and compassion, but my heart was unmoved. Amazingly, I was middle-aged before I caught on to this fact about myself. By then, I was blessed by the fellowship of recovery, friends who told me the truth, and a wonderful second marriage after losing my first wife to cancer.

Underneath it all, whether we know it or not, we are all vulnerable. My heart has unfurled over these many years. Now, wherever there are people, I feel our kinship.

***

Galen Tinder grew up and went to college in Massachusetts and has spent most of his adult life in New Jersey. Galen is retired from a career in ministry, counseling, and consulting. He now spends much of his time volunteering for hospice and recovering communities, exercising outdoors, and conducting and writing about Structured Life Reviews.

48

Delivery: My Sequel to Labor

by Joanne McEnroy

"The child must know that he is a miracle. That since the beginning of the world, there hasn't been, and until the end of the world, there will not be, another child like him." – Pablo Casals

On May 4, 1987, at approximately 11:34 a.m., the "stork" delivered our child to JFK International airport. We had waited a lifetime for this beautiful baby boy from South Korea. Daniel was almost four months old when he came home with us. Before that, I had only a single photo that I carried with me wherever I went. I would prop it up so that I could watch him, and he could see me, throughout the day. I was nesting, I knew—prepping for his arrival as I had for the last fifteen years of our marriage. I couldn't remember a time when I did not want a child. But nothing could have readied me for the moment when that baby was placed in my arms.

"Wait!" I wanted to shout, "You've made a terrible mistake!" Even after a full year's investigation, reference checks, and reams of paperwork regaling our family histories, motivations, and values, I felt woefully unprepared for that moment. When the social worker who had cared for our son during his twenty-four-hour trip handed him to me, I was nothing short of terrified.

"Congratulations, Mommy and Daddy! Your son smiled the whole way home." She went on to say, "And it's been my experience that how they make this journey is how they journey through life."

As it turned out, she was right.

That's the story of how our family was born, but it is not the story of how our family grew. Seems it was not just the excitement of motherhood that had me feeling nauseous over the next few weeks.

I had given up reacting to every nuance in my body, abandoning thermometers and charts for feeding times and diapers. But no sooner had I started to admit that I just might be pregnant, I lost yet another child. This one hit me harder than the others. I remember sobbing one day, "What kind of God would want to spoil my happiness like this? I want Him to stop messing with me!"

By the following summer, He was at it again—determined, I suppose, to finally get it right.

Kevin was born after thirty-four hard hours of labor, an eight-pound, eleven-ounce testimony to the wisdom imparted by the social worker after our first son's arrival. Kevin's journey may have been different, but his disposition mimicked his trip. Kevin was the yin to Danny's yang, the Jekyll to his Hyde. We called them "God's gift and God's sense of humor," and they were adorable, my mismatched pair!

Though we never encountered any real prejudices, we did experience our fair share of very stupid questions. But our feeling was that these questions arose more from ignorance than insensitivity. We handled most of them with humor and aplomb—except for Kevin, who got suspended from the school bus the third week of first grade for punching Anthony Cimino in the face.

"I kept telling him Danny was Korean, but he just kept calling him 'China Eyes'. Every day, every day! What else did you want me to do?!"

We would spend the next two decades answering that question with Kevin. But curiously, Dan rode that same bus with Anthony Cimino for two years before his brother joined him and never said a word about it to us. When I finally broached it with him, my wise-beyond-his-years third grader said, "He's a jerk, Mom. I just figured it said a lot more about him than me, so I ignored it."

How did I get these two very different children? Yet they are allies and best friends. I found out only recently that in college, they conned bartenders out of free beers by asking them to "guess which two of us are brothers."

My favorite picture of our boys shows Danny as the best man at Kevin's wedding. They are doubled over in laughter after realizing—about an hour before it was time to walk down the aisle—that one of the groomsmen had been delivered the wrong color suit. This photo captures who they are and who they have been: a dynamic duo, loyal, connected, loving, and filled with a sense of humor as crazy as ours.

While Dan now lives across the pond (single, intent on filling every page of his passport), Kevin resides happily in suburbia with his wife, two children, and a puppy. They talk almost every day, connected by a bond that is richer, thicker, and deeper than any I have ever known.

And their humor lives on. The first thing Dan sent his newborn niece was a pacifier that made it look like she was making a duck face. "For all of the selfies she's gonna be posting online," he taunted his already overprotective brother.

There is no greater gift than the gift of my boys, their love for each other, their sense of family, and their humor.

Except perhaps, for this. Not long ago, my son confided to me that he and his wife would love to consider adoption. "Our family was really cool, Mom, and I want my kids to experience that." Me too, Kevin. Me, too.

***

Retired from a four-decade career in teaching, Joanne is sharing life healthily with her husband and family. She's been "GAB'bing" for four years, first as a student and more recently as a facilitator. She loves the story experiences shared with amazing groups of writers. Joanne feels blessed to be a snowbird in Florida but calls Long Island her home.

49

How I Learned That People Are Supposed to Love

by Jerry Waxler

My parents, children of Jewish refugees, had not yet figured out how to fit into the melting pot of America. Unfortunately, neither had I.

I had no interest in throwing or catching balls with boys in the alley behind my Philadelphia row home. Instead, I turned to books. When I wasn't studying or reading, I was stocking shelves or waiting on customers at my dad's drugstore. I thought I had figured out the path to adulthood: just stay busy and everything will work out.

Time passed and I was an eighteen-year-old college student in Madison, Wisconsin. Suddenly I was drowning in an ocean of thirty-thousand students, the vast majority from ethnic groups different from mine. I had no idea how to relate.

When anti-war protests began, I was drawn to the groups of people screaming in unison. It reminded me of the togetherness people must feel at a sports stadium. I joined in, shouting on behalf of the team that wanted no war. It was satisfying for the moment, but I still didn't know how to have an ordinary conversation.

Other aspects of the counterculture promised a sense of belonging. I dressed in the uniform: long hair, blue jeans, and a work shirt. "Hey, look at me, I look just like you! We're in this together, right?" Alone in my room, smoking marijuana and listening to the latest Beatles album, I felt like part of some big movement.

Then why was I still so lonely?

After college things got even worse. Moving to Berkeley, California—the very epicenter of the counterculture—I went weeks without speaking to anyone. My ability to connect with people was seriously broken.

Then, by grace, luck, or sheer desperation, I latched on to a spiritual path based on the principle that "God is love." Love!? This was new. For the first time, I hoped that I might someday figure out how to connect with others.

Driven by a mission to learn how to love, I stumbled on a group of people in Pennsylvania, not too far from where I grew up. Everyone got along, and I got along with everyone. It was such a radical departure—I had friends all the time.

We were companions, allies, supporters. We went to the movies together. Ate dinner together. Since there were about thirty of us, we celebrated a birthday every few weeks. We sang together in a choir. Rode bikes in packs on country roads. Went on vacations to the Cayman Islands and Nantucket.

We also helped each other survive the game of life. Over time we became more competent: getting jobs, starting businesses, forming relationships. Without even realizing such a thing existed, I'd somehow stumbled upon a halfway house for aspiring adults.

In my thirties, I realized that I was close to people in my group but still distant from everyone else. So I began to see a therapist.

Paying someone to listen so carefully nurtured my soul. I loved therapy so much that I went to grad school at the age of fifty to become a therapist myself. While grad school pushed me further out of isolation than I ever thought possible, by the time I graduated I still had not mastered the art of opening my heart. I needed to keep growing.

One of the lessons that kept coming up was the way words offer a pathway into emotions. To learn more, I sought the company of wordsmiths. At a nonprofit writing club in Bucks County, Pennsylvania, our shared interest created an instant bond. I had found my tribe. When that organization locked its doors, the writers retreated to their homes. I was heartbroken.

Back to searching again, I realized that if I wanted to be around writers, I would need to form my own group. Impossible! I had never led anything before, but soon discovered a hidden passion for teaching. I began teaching self-help and psychology to writers.

When I came across the memoir genre, all the psychological techniques and jargon dropped away. As each person shared a small glimpse into their attempts to grow up and fit in, I witnessed the profound synergism between words, revealing, and healing. Not only was I defeating my own loneliness, I was helping others defeat theirs.

Groups of people from every background imaginable arrived at my classes with the usual human attitude: "we're different because our experiences are different." They left seeing how our unique experiences make us fascinating to each other.

I have managed to live long enough to participate in a new movement—we are protesting separation.

Some may see it as ironic that reading and writing books has offered a resolution to my struggles with isolation and otherness. But humans have always turned to stories for a higher perspective.

I see the Memoir Revolution as a natural, beautiful progression of a human culture desperately trying to know itself.

Admittedly, memoir groups differ from the usual expressions of love in families and friendships. Fortunately, after a lifetime of learning to open my heart and listen, I've grown in those areas too. Love through hugs. Love through empathy. Love through stories. I think I'm finally getting the hang of this "love" thing. Thanks to that, I belong everywhere.

***

Jerry Waxler, M.S., speaks, coaches and teaches about how life story writing awakens self-understanding. Jerry's book Memoir Revolution *celebrates this social trend that heals, connects and inspires. His memoir* Thinking My Way to the End of the World *describes his own coming of age through the chaotic sixties. Jerry lives in Quakertown, Pennsylvania.*

Ready to write your story?

Learn how to write your life stories and connect with other life story writers by joining a Guided Autobiography program in your neighborhood or online.

To browse instructors and available classes, visit:
www.GuidedAutobiography.com

Acknowledgments

This book is the work of a few side-tracked members of the global Guided Autobiography community whose main objective is to help people write down the stories of their lives. Thank you to the instructors who passionately pursue that incredible mission, which gets way too little publicity and is much more life-changing than these humble pages.

To everyone who contributed their story without asking for anything in return, you are what makes this community a force for positive global change. To Galen Tinder and Val Perry for adding their wisdom to the reader team. And to our proofreader extraordinaire Briana Valadao, who is probably annoyed with me for starting this sentence with "and."

We'd like to thank Emma Fulenwider for shepherding the authors, and Sarah White and Peggy Rosen for shepherding Emma.

Lastly, we are forever indebted to Dr. Cheryl Svensson for carrying the bright torch of the Birren Method so that the world may see each other more clearly.

Also by the Birren Center Press

ONWARD! True Life Stories of Challenges, Choices & Change

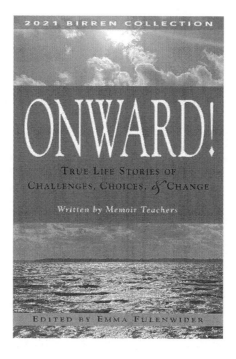

Made in the USA
Middletown, DE
09 November 2022

14485369R00120